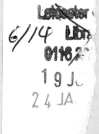

Knit Back in Time

A RotoVision Book

Published in 2013 by Search Press Ltd.
Wellwood, North Farm Road,
Tunbridge Wells,
Kent TN2 3DR

This book is produced by
RotoVision SA
114 Western Rd
Hove
BND 1DD
Copyright © 2012 RotoVision

ISBN 978-1-84448-904-6

Commissioning Editor: Isheeta Mustafi
Design concept: Emily Portnoi
Art Editor: Jennifer Osborne
Artworking: Sarah Howerd | Sideways14
Stylist: Emily Inglis (woodenhillvintage.com)
Cover design: Emily Portnoi
Hats on pp. 7, 23, 60 and 131 supplied by Shelley Zetuni
at Gold Dust Millinery Studio

Photography: Ivan Jones
Illustrations: Peters & Zabransky Ltd

Knit Back in Time

INCLUDES TECHNIQUES FOR UPDATING VINTAGE PATTERNS AND RETRO-STYLING MODERN PATTERNS

Geraldine Warner

SEARCH PRESS

Contents

Updating vintage patterns

Why I love vintage knits

WHAT DOES 'VINTAGE' MEAN?

Vintage is a fairly general term that has become popular in recent years and is used to encompass just about anything over thirty years old. For the context of this book I am using 'vintage' to cover the period spanning the early 1900s up until the 1960s. The reason I stop there is that by that point knitting patterns were providing several different size options and using yarns and yarn thicknesses that are more familiar to us today.

The later designs, to be honest, do not appeal to me as much. You can still find some wonderful patterns from the 1970s, and do not forget that the 1980s, although guilty of many knitted crimes, also drew heavily on the 1950s, so you may find some familiar vintage styling creeping into the occasional interesting pattern.

WHY KNIT VINTAGE?

Everyone has a story about how they learnt to knit – mine is pretty straightforward and unexceptional, and possibly a lot like yours: my mum and both grandmothers had the patience and foresight to teach me. No fuss, no talk about legacy, inheritance or creativity – it was just a part of my upbringing. WWII was influential in their lives and tales of their experiences were inherently woven into the knitting lessons. My mum had also hung on to her collection of 1950s *Vogue Knitting* books along with some of the dresses and blouses knitted from them and somehow they seeped into my consciousness.

I love this link to the people in my family, this maternal woolly cord that still connects us although they are all long gone, and I enjoy the possibility that I might be knitting from a pattern they used themselves.

Individuality

Nowadays, thanks to technological advances, clothes are mass-produced cheaply in faraway countries with unknown provenance and thousands are wearing that great 'individual' top you bought last week. Although this has given choices to many where there were none before, we also have the choice to explore a different route and there are things we can do to assert our individuality in the face of such homogenisation.

Technology means that we have access to a vast range of materials, equipment and creative ideas. We can make pretty much whatever we want and celebrate the days when detail, individuality and quality were valued. What better way than to raid the best of the designs from the past and re-create them yourself?

Bringing history to life

Whenever I finish a garment knitted from a vintage pattern and try it on I get an enormous kick – it is very possible that that particular design has not seen the light of day for sixty or seventy years and here I stand, in my self-made garment, breathing life back into it – how often do you get the chance to directly interact with history in that way?

The patterns are fascinating items in themselves, the notes their previous owners have made in the margins, their names pencilled at the top, the creases where they stored them, the stamps of long-gone yarn shops... each pattern has its own story to tell if you listen hard enough, and you can add your own part to that story by bringing it back to life.

This 1950s pattern combines bold stripes with an unusual sleeve design and fitted waist.

The thing to bear in mind is that knitted fabric is just that: fabric. When I was a child I used to make clothes for my dolls with no concept of cut, drape or fit – I just cut out shapes that seemed to fit the right dimensions and off I went, unrestrained by rules or fear of messing up.

When we knit, we are creating our own fabric to create shapes that we then sew together. (It was common in the 1930s for knitters to create knitted pieces using sewing patterns as a guide.) As long as you know the required measurements

and you can increase or decrease, then you should have no problems. Obviously it also helps to have an understanding of how your yarn, needle and stitch choices affect your garment, but this book will, I hope, help you to understand more about this.

HAVE CONFIDENCE!

If you have picked this book up I am going to assume that you are a knitter who finds yourself drawn to vintage patterns and fashions, but are worried about how to approach and adapt them. I will also make the assumption that you have a certain amount of knitting knowledge (basic/intermediate) but you really do not have to be a complete expert. On the contrary, it can sometimes be an advantage if you are coming at this with only a little knitted baggage and few rules to unpick.

This book is written in the spirit of experimentation – mistakes will be made but, armed with patience and determination, lessons will be learnt, your confidence will grow and eventually the world will become your knitted oyster.

The ribbed stitch pattern in this 1940s cardigan ensures a tight, elastic fit.

Using this book

The book is divided into two parts: the first section takes you through the process of finding and assessing a vintage pattern, choosing an appropriate yarn, deciding what components you need to change and understanding how to change them. These are all the basics you will ever need to knit from a vintage pattern. We will be looking at one particular garment knitted from start to finish, step by step, as an example of the process, and to help you with ideas about how to approach your own pattern.

The second section is a more adventurous approach to knitting a vintage-styled garment. If you like the idea of 'pimping' more recent patterns, we will be looking at how to take a modern pattern and adapt it to fit your vintage requirements. We include patterns for vintage elements such as sleeves, collars and other details, and once again we will be using a particular garment as an example.

This is not a basic techniques guide; this book is intended to give you the confidence to experiment and explore and bring some beautiful creations back to life.

Frequent reference pages

Here is a list of pages I think you will find most useful and will return to again and again, with blank spaces for you to fill in your own notes.

Section one

Section two

Sock yarn is a good substitute for some of the finer yarns found in vintage patterns.

A guide to twentieth-century knitting fashions

Women's fashion in the West underwent dramatic changes during the twentieth century. The following brief guide to fashion, undergarments and shapes from the last century might help you decide which era you would like to knit from, and give you a rough idea of what sort of shape you are aiming for. It may even help you to date your pattern where there is doubt.

PRE-1920s: FROM CORSETS TO SUFFRAGETTES

At the start of the twentieth century, the Victorian fashion for torturous body constriction and restriction continued. Whalebone still had a firm clutch on fashionable figures, this time in the form of the 'health' or S-shape corset that thrust the female figure forwards into a bizarre 'S' shape. But thankfully this unnatural shape soon fell out of fashion, not least because it was shown to distort the spine.

Also, female fans of the Arts and Crafts movement were flouting rules about fashion, favouring empire lines and more free-flowing, corset-free shapes – a natural shape that would eventually prove to last. Fashion magazines were beginning to laud the freedom of movement, and sportswear for women was becoming acceptable.

As the corset line sank to below the breast – by 1913 most corsets were only 2in (5cm) above the waist – it became necessary to cover the bust, so the original corset covers (or camisoles, as they became known) took on a new role that would form a more comfortable basis for undergarments in the 1920s and launch hundreds of underwear knitting patterns.

The start of WWI in July 1914 saw knitting go from a diverting pastime to a worldwide craze. Women were knitting scarves, mittens, helmets and support garments for soldiers. But tension (gauge) advice still had not made it into knitting pattern guidelines, so strangely outsized garments became the subject of popular jokes.

By this time, designer Coco Chanel was making her fashionable mark from her second shop in Deauville (following her first in Paris in 1913), featuring lines of knitted sportswear. She forged ahead with her trademark look: a much looser fit more suited to the modern woman's lifestyle, which actually enabled her to walk with ease.

An advertisement for an S-shaped 'health' corset from 1897.

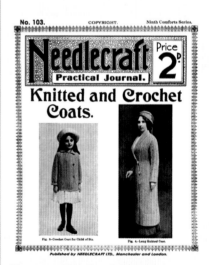

The cover of *Needlecraft Practical Journal: Knitted & Crochet Coats*, c. 1912

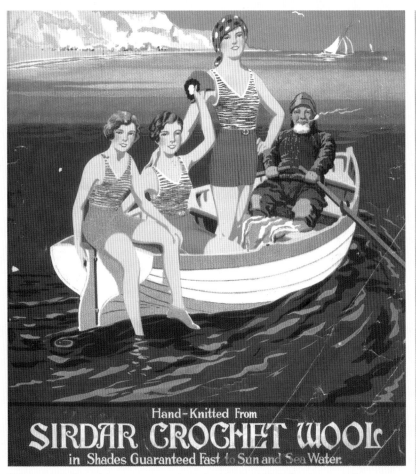

Hand-Knitted From
SIRDAR CROCHET WOOL
in Shades Guaranteed Fast to Sun and Sea Water.

This pattern reflected the growing popularity (and acceptability) of active sports for women.

1920s: THE DAPPER FLAPPER

The 'flapper' epitomized the age: free-spirited and hedonistic, she needed clothes to suit her new-found freedom. Skirts became shorter, exercise for women became acceptable and popular leisure pursuits became more active than ever before.

The age of informal dressing dawned, including chemises, tunics and slip-on frocks, plus the rise of the jumper and casual three-piece suit. Chanel and avant-garde newcomer Elsa Schiaparelli (known as La Schiap) did all they could to ensure the knitted suit and sweater were here to stay, and combined elegantly cut garments with the most dazzling artistic designs of the day. La Schiap introduced a collection of knitwear in 1928 that included the instantly famous bowknot jumper (made with a double-layered stitch technique used by Armenian refugees).

Underwear & sportswear
Undergarments now had to streamline the figure into a shapeless silhouette, squashing any contours or bumps, resulting in the requisite boyish appearance. Flattening underwear such as the corselette and the exotically named corslo-pantalon-chemise gave the body a more tubular appearance.

Sportswear became increasingly popular: John Smedley launched his 'tennis shirt', later to be known as the polo shirt, which was to form the basis of many a popular knitting pattern in the 1930s.

Some dazzling patterns for knitted bathing suits appeared around this time too, and since underwear had become less restrictive and more a cover-up formality, patterns for fine-wool all-in-ones or separate vest and knickers were ubiquitous for the next fifteen years or so, until developments in synthetics and elastic made even the finest hand-knitted fabrics almost obsolete.

In 1925, the Duke of Windsor was depicted on canvas in a now-famous portrait wearing his golfing outfit, which included a Fair Isle jumper. Not only did this boost the Outer-Hebridean knitting industry, the influence of that picture was to continue well into the next twenty to thirty years, prompting a resurgence of Fair Isle's popularity in knitting, particularly during WWII.

By the late 1920s, hemlines were starting to drop and the boyish look was receding; the existence of the bust was acknowledged and the feminine waist was making itself known again. Underwear was not about to make a return to its more excessive restrictions, but gentle curves reappeared and were quietly enhanced.

1930s: LONGER AND STRONGER

Following the Wall Street Crash in 1929, the previous decade suddenly seemed frivolous and decadent – exit the flapper, enter the sombre working girl. The repercussions of this shift were felt through the fashion world and, true to the old adage, hemlines dropped along with the economy. Women aspired to be tall and slender.

Schiaparelli's surrealist influence was particularly noticeable in many of the knitting patterns over the next decade: geometric shapes, faux neckties, scarves and belts became popular features towards the end of the 1920s and carried into patterns of the 1930s.

One of the many fashion by-products of the Hollywood age was what we now think of as an unassuming garment. Women were seen on screen in the bedroom, but of course they had to look simultaneously glamorous, attractive and modest – enter the bedjacket in glorious lacy forms, some with voluminous sleeves trimmed with ribbons and marabou. The trend lasted long into the 1950s and some of these stunning patterns are good enough for evening blouses today.

The exaggerated shoulder was big news in the early 1930s, and it grew to great heights in many different forms, swiftly followed by sleeve shapes that appeared in more and more extravagant iterations.

The working woman managed to combine sleek sophistication with toned-down touches of high fashion, and sometimes witty glamour.

An early 1930s pattern for the Cranston Jumper showcases an inventive approach to sleeve design.

Taking their cue from the still popular Art Deco influence, small yet daring details cropped up in the inventive knitting patterns of the time to raise her outfit above mundane practicality: contrast collars and sleeves; geometric shapes, stripes, chevrons and diagonals in bold colour combinations; scarf-collars and cravats; and slimline dresses and skirts – all of which were echoed in knitted or crocheted accessories such as bags, gloves and hats. Embroidered touches were popular too: flowers and monograms made up of French knots, satin stitch and lazy daisy stitch could all make knitwear more individual, and the celebrated material Bakelite found a new form in novelty buttons.

Magazine giant Condé Nast capitalised on the knitting boom and started up *Vogue Knitting* magazine in 1932, the same year that Patons and Baldwins launched their own knitting magazine title, *Stitchcraft*, which produced wonderfully innovative, elegant and exciting knitting patterns.

Underwear

Developments in garment construction and materials influenced undergarments as well. A lady's 'stays' were still an important part of her wardrobe, although they rarely contained whalebone or metal supports any longer. The Dunlop Rubber Company developed elastic thread (or Lastex as it was known), an element that was to prove revolutionary to underwear during this period. The girdle became a more comfortable (although still pretty solid) option and the 'bra' first appeared as a separate entity, worn with a tight corset belt and cami-knickers.

The accommodating panty girdle conveniently nipped in the waist and flattened the hips. There was still a more relaxed approach to underwear: many magazines contained sewing patterns for making lingerie. Underwear was repeatedly darned, patched and mended, techniques that were particularly useful during WWII.

An underwear advertisement from a 1936 magazine for a 'slymlastik' corset proves that marketing has not changed much over the years.

1940s: BEAUTY TURNS TO DUTY

The early to mid-1940s were a fashion leveller, particularly in Europe – out went the escapist fantasies and in came the clothes of necessity. Even in the wealthier families it became unfashionable to demonstrate excess and it was not considered appropriate to wear finer garments, even if you had them.

Fashion became limited by restrictions – Parisian design disappeared under the cloak of German occupation in 1940, and did not re-emerge until its first post-liberation collection in the autumn of 1944.

Shortages of fabric and factory requisitions meant that fashion became utilitarian: a box- or square-shouldered suit with padded shoulders, accompanied by matching skirt just below the knee became the look of the day, often paired with a plain blouse or knitted jumper underneath.

Turbans started out as practical headwear for factory workers that kept the wearers' hair out of machinery, but evolved into everyday wear for those who had no time or materials to whip up a fine hair-do. Many turban knitting patterns still survive, and they have become iconic items themselves.

Making yarn go further

Knitters worldwide had to be thrifty and innovative with their limited supply of yarns, so knitted fashion drew on elements from recent years: the favoured high waist in the 1930s conveniently meant that shorter jumpers used less wool, for example. The Fair Isle jumper made popular in the 1920s also came back into vogue as you could use odds and ends of different colours – especially useful when it came to unravelling old garments.

Many patterns could be found for blouse fronts with a netted or fabric back to be worn under suit jackets, another wool-saving exercise. Although possibly regarded as frivolous, lacy and open stitches could also, potentially, stretch the yarn further, and had the advantage of turning a plain design into an attractive evening outfit. Magazines of the time were full of embroidery motifs and ways to brighten up your wardrobe using decorative hand-worked embellishments.

Post-war changes

High-end fashion saw a return to more opulent creations as early as 1947 with Christian Dior's lavish and controversial 'New Look' collection. Designer Mainbocher had relocated from Paris to New York at the start of the war. His shapely pre-war vision came out of hibernation and saw the hourglass figure become established as the ultimate feminine statement (aided by his invention, the Mainbocher corset). As national supply restrictions gradually eased up, fabric and yarn were used in increasing quantities.

The practical 1940s turban became a classic fashion accessory.

Shortage of different materials meant that the popularity of knitted underwear continued during WWII, providing much-needed warmth.

1950s: FULL CIRCLE

By 1950 it was official: the tiny waist was back. Freed from fabric production constraints, skirts became fuller and so did busts, both of which handily accentuated a small waist. Figure-hugging V-necks elongated the torso, accentuated the cleavage and made a neat triangular shape ending at the waist, then flared out dramatically over the hips into a full, below-the-knee skirt, or clung to the legs in a tight-fitting pencil skirt.

Knitwear went from necessity to asset and an outburst of knitting patterns appeared with ever more stunning designs. No longer did you have to unravel your old knits; a whole new world of yarn was available in every colour as yarn broke free from rationing.

Demure, fine-knitted, tailored shapes hugged the figure, with *Vogue Knitting* leading the field with increasingly spectacular hand-knitted designs. Accessories and haberdashery flooded back on to the market, and sequins, appliqué and beadwork were to be found adorning simple twinsets and cardigans. The fashionable shirt-dress was echoed to great effect in knitted form.

Boat-shaped necklines, whimsical yet demure off-the-shoulder numbers, boleros and shrugs all gave daytime outfits a night-time appeal. The dolman, raglan and magyar sleeves became popular, making the top half slightly more voluminous to emphasise – you guessed it – that all-important tiny waist. The cap sleeve also accentuated the top of the torso 'triangle'.

Underwear

That tiny waist came with its usual cost – the corset was welcomed back into the underwear drawer (albeit elasticised and rubberised rather than whaleboned and laced), along with net petticoats and structured brassieres. Spirella, Triumph and Berlei all did everything they could to help the public get an hourglass shape, producing range after range of all-in-one girdles with integral bras, separate hip girdles, 'waspies' and padded uplifting bras. Dresses even came with their own built-in boned bodices, and the strapless bra appeared to enhance beautiful, shoulderless evening dresses.

Signs of the future

The end of the 1950s saw the return of a simpler shape – change was in the air yet again. The efforts of leading fashion designers Cristóbal Balenciaga and Hubert de Givenchy to free the female form from corsets with designs such as the chemise and 'Sack' dress were to pay off and lead the way to the hip sixties. Patterns for chunky ski or sports jumpers caught on.

Fashion found a new, younger audience in the rise of teenagers who wanted to break free from the restrictions of the previous generation's fashions, preferring a return to a more relaxed, comfortable form.

Knitted dresses and suits showed off a small waist, especially when teamed with a full skirt. Note the beautiful stitch in this dress pattern.

Knitted underwear was soon to become obsolete, but beautiful patterns were still popular during the first half of the 1950s.

1960s: TO INFINITY & BEYOND

The old shapes and traditions persisted for a couple of years before they were rejected with a finality that forbade their return. Youth had a voice for the first time since the 1920s, and it was shouting loud and proud – street fashion started to influence high fashion.

The mod mode took street fashion by storm: the post-war years had proved grey and lean, and the 'rebellious' values of the 1950s rocker seemed quaint, old-fashioned and provincial by now: the mods wanted something harder, sharper and faster.

Male mods pared down their look, taking their lead from sharp-cut Italian styles and fine knitwear. Female mods, in a move echoing the 1920s, dressed androgynously in shapeless or low-waisted tunics and shift dresses, male button-down shirts or polo shirts, sporting short haircuts and even shorter skirts.

High fashion grew to love this look and by the mid-1960s had adapted it for its own stylish purposes. *Vogue Knitting* No. 67 from 1965 features a tattersall-check tunic photographed by 1960s icon David Bailey, and a fantastic wool supplement from 1967 features patterns for a tunic jumper with chequered shorts and a boldly coloured take on a Fair Isle jersey with matching beret and socks.

The hippy culture
Textured knits became popular in the 1960s as the hippy culture spread its wings; garments were trimmed with crochet and knitted lace, and the crochet mini dress was a must-have. Unlike previous decades when any lacy outergarment had to be lined or worn over opaque undergarments, underwear became optional for the first time. Transparency was acceptable, even giving a glimpse of the previously unmentionable.

Underwear
Bras were either built to be incredibly lightweight to give a 'hardly there' effect, or simply not worn at all. All-in-ones did still exist to give a smoothing effect where necessary: body stockings and light panty-corselettes made from Lycra were available, and tights took over from stockings for the first time. Fashion would never be the same again.

Textured knits adapted to suit 'Swinging Sixties' styles.

Freedom of movement was essential (although shaping underwear was still in vogue) and innovations in elastics saw the end of knitted underwear.

Right: This gorgeous 1940s jumper is knitted using original 2-ply yarn, which shows off the lace pattern stitch to perfection.

3

Industric
Housewiv

who fill in t
moments of comparat
leisure by plain or fancy knitt
will do well to insist that the Beeh
Trade Mark appears on every skein
packet of wool they buy.

The "BEE___VE" Bra___

Updating vintage patterns

Finding & assessing your pattern

This is the fun part! If you are reading this book you may already have your eye on a vintage pattern or two; maybe you have picked up a pile from a jumble sale, inherited a stash from a relative or found something on the internet. But before you get too excited, it is important to assess the pattern carefully to make sure you will be able to use it.

FINDING YOUR PATTERN

The boom in vintage fashion, combined with a knitting resurrection, means that finding your perfect pattern should be an enjoyable task.

Inheritance & word of mouth

Perhaps the most satisfying patterns are the ones you have inherited from previous generations, friends of the family or neighbours – it is nice to have that personal link, so I would recommend that as the best place to start. You may find out a little bit of the history behind the patterns and the person who originally knitted them, which adds an extra dimension to your knitting pleasure. Spread the word that you are on the lookout for old patterns – you will be surprised how many people respond.

Charity shops & jumble sales

It is becoming harder to find some of the more outstanding vintage knitting patterns in shops or at sales. As vintage knitting has become more popular, knitters are less likely to want to part with any remarkable patterns, preferring to keep them or sell them through specialists. However, I still have a good rummage around in case I come across something, so do not let it deter you. These sources are also a good source for the patterns used in the second half of the book.

Vintage shops

Chances are if you are into vintage fashion you will enjoy spending more time than is good for you in vintage and antique shops. I would not say that vintage knitting patterns are abundant, but if you do find yourself wandering the aisles and shelves without any success it is always worth asking the owner if they have any hidden away. That same owner might also keep an eye open for you if you are lucky.

Above: Magazines and knitting booklets give you a great background to the era in which they were printed.

Left: An amazing number of books and patterns have survived from the last century.

Websites

Internet auction sites such as eBay are a good place to start. The increasing popularity of vintage knitting means that prices have gone up, but you can still find some bargains. I think even the pricier patterns are worthwhile when you consider their age and what the end product is. Do not forget to look out for magazines and knitting booklets – although they are likely to be a bit more expensive, they will be worth it in terms of the wealth of extra delights you will find, including accessories, adverts and numerous lovely patterns.

The appearance of reproduction patterns has increased considerably over the last couple of years, so if you are after an original make sure you have thoroughly read through the item description before you buy.

There are also a few vintage knitting websites, some of which give away free vintage patterns – a good search should reward you. I have listed some in 'Useful resources' on page 160. I find some of them particularly useful for earlier patterns from the early 1900s or 1920s, which are very rare and hard to get hold of.

Bestway's 'Tea-Time Jumper' from the mid-1940s is typical of the era's styling, with its box-top sleeves and deep-ribbed welt.

ASSESSING YOUR PATTERN STYLE

This is where your investigations start to assess the strengths and shortcomings of your pattern.

The first rule of assessing a vintage pattern is the most obvious but often most overlooked – will it look flattering on me? It is easy to get carried away with how great a 1940s blouse looks on the model. You find yourself getting swept up in the romantic notion of the era it was designed in, fall in love with it, adapt it, knit it, only to find it does not complement your body type.

The whole point is to revel in these fashions and feel good when you are wearing them, not banish them to a drawer where they languish. You are going to have to use the practical side of your imagination and decide where it will fit into your wardrobe, and even your lifestyle. Ask yourself a few questions before you dive in:

- Will it suit your body shape? Do exaggerated leg-of-mutton sleeves really have a place in your life? Is that empire-line top going to flatter your ample bust? Be realistic and apply the same rules that you would to the rest of your wardrobe.

- What will you be wearing it with? You may only have the odd vintage piece of clothing, maybe preferring to dress your retro pieces up with some more modern accessories. Trouser and skirt waistbands are considerably lower than they once were, but be aware that there is only a certain amount of length you can add to a vintage garment before it loses its original vintage proportions and starts to look very different.

- Will the original style still work if it is sized up?

- Will the pattern really work with modern styles? Is it just that it complements the model's shape (particularly as it may have some artificial help from the underwear of the time), her hairstyle sets it off and that pencil skirt works so well with it?

PATTERN INSTRUCTIONS

We will be looking at how to read your original pattern and re-create a fairly accurately sized picture of it in 'Deconstruct to reconstruct' on page 32, but at this stage it is important to identify any potential queries or problems. You might want to make some initial notes to highlight latent obstacles.

If this is your first time adapting a vintage pattern and you do not have a tremendous amount of knitting experience, make sure you find something that does not, for example, have a complicated stitch pattern or colourwork so you can focus purely on the adaptation.

If you are really set on a particular pattern, practise knitting up the stitch it uses until you are really comfortable with it, then knit up a few swatches to check that you are happy with the results.

Next you need to complete an in-depth look at all the pattern's elements so you can decide if the pattern is one you will be able to find appropriate yarn for, easily adapt and understand.

In this section we will be looking at a specific set of instructions for 'A Tea-Time Jumper' by Bestway, Leaflet No. 605. This is a British 1940s pattern, probably printed sometime just after WWII, since it is a good deal smaller than the 1930s patterns and the quality of the paper is not great (the lingering result of rationing).

The yarns used in this 1940s jumper design are vintage and the colours reflect the subdued wartime pallet, brightened up with a few flashes of jade green.

Description

Not all patterns include a description, but where there is one you might find some clues to the type of yarn you will need. Ours includes the information: 'Airy fairy but with all the warmth of wool – this little jumper shows you just how feminine and charming knitting designs can be.'

Materials

Next are the materials, which are listed as:

- 7oz of 'Golden Eagle' Lustre Suede or Suede, 3-ply

- 1 pair each of No. 10 and No. 12 knitting needles.

This is often the point where people give up – how do you know what Golden Eagle Lustre was? Or how much 7oz equates to?

We will go into this in more detail in the upcoming sections, but you can find some more clues at first glance. Have a look at the garment image, how it drapes; it has a 'soft' look to it, possibly even a slight sheen, so this style would definitely suit a delicate, soft yarn.

If you did not already know this was a 3-ply yarn, you would have another clue in the needle sizes. Sizes 10 and 12 are the US equivalents of sizes 3 and 1 (see 'Needle sizes', page 162), so this is definitely at the finer end of the yarn spectrum.

Tension (gauge)

This is a vital key to unlocking the pattern. Not all vintage patterns will give you tension guidance, although it was becoming more standard by the 1940s, and even a large percentage of 1930s patterns will include it. If the pattern does not include a tension guide, it is by no means the end of the story, but you will need a lot more guesswork.

In this example pattern, we are given a tension guide as follows:

After pressing, 7 sts to 1in in width and 10 rows to 1in in depth measured over the pattern section worked on No. 10 needles.

This provides you with another clue to your eventual yarn choice. Knitting 7 stitches and 10 rows to the inch is going to produce a fine fabric that will show off the lacy pattern beautifully.

Measurements

From this section you will be able to establish whether or not (and how much) you will need to size up (or down if you are lucky).

Abbreviations

Are there any abbreviations in the pattern guide that you are unfamiliar with? Have a look through the pattern instructions themselves to make sure that everything is explained in the abbreviation key, or you are going to need to do a bit of research to make sure you understand what the pattern is describing.

Instructions

Read through the instructions thoroughly, step by step, to identify any problems. If you come across an indecipherable enigma, turn to your swatch and try it out on a test piece, or pick up your notebook and try to sketch it out. Vintage patterns can contain errors so sometimes you will need to trust your instincts when you think something is not quite right.

Do not forget the vital part at the end, the 'Make up' section. You can find all the clues you need here about the construction of your garment and you may even be able to fill in some gaps that were not clear from the main instructions.

Pro tip

If you are committed to trying a pattern you do not completely understand, try talking to other knitters. For example, the knitter's dream community website Ravelry (see 'Useful resources', page 160), is a great place to ask for help.

SEE ALSO Taking your measurements, page 30, Deconstruct to reconstruct, page 32, Finding yarn to suit your pattern, page 42

Our revised 'Tea-Time Jumper' works well in a silk/wool mix.

Tension & tension swatching

When you are knitting from vintage patterns, you are invariably dealing with unknown original yarns, so a tension swatch is not only helpful when you are selecting an appropriate modern yarn, but also essential to decode the pattern if you are intending to re-size or adapt it. No matter how many times you knit from a vintage pattern, this must ALWAYS be an important part of your planning.

WHAT IS A TENSION (GAUGE) SWATCH?

Tension swatches are knitted to establish how many stitches and rows you get to the inch, from which you can then calculate the overall measurements of the garment by using a very simple calculation: desired width × tension.

For example, if you want to knit a piece that is 15in (37.5cm) wide, and your tension swatch came up 7 stitches to the inch (2.5cm), then the number of stitches you need to cast on (bind on) would be 15 × 7 = 105 stitches.

Pro tip

If your original pattern does not give you a tension swatch, you can knit your swatch up and work out how closely it matches the measurements given. (Most patterns will give you at least one or two width measurements to work from.)

These three swatches show how different weights of yarn and needle sizes affect the tension. They are, from left to right: 4-ply yarn on 3.5mm (US 4) needles, 8-ply yarn on 4mm (US 6) needles and 12-ply yarn on 6mm (US 10) needles.

SEE ALSO Taking your measurements, page 30, Calculating yardage & weight, page 48, Needle sizes, page 162

HOW TO CHECK YOUR TENSION (GAUGE) SWATCH

1. Once you have chosen a suitable yarn (see page 42), cast on 30 stitches and knit about 40 rows (or whatever is recommended on the yarn ball band – modern yarns usually suggest a tension swatch measuring 4in (10cm) of the main stitch used in the garment.

2. Pin out your knitted square on to a flat surface (an ironing board will do), making sure the edges are straight. Pin it to some graph paper for a guide.

3. Place a pin or tacking stitch at the point from which you intend to measure then measure a 3in (8cm) square in the centre of the knitting (rigid tape measures or rulers are easiest to use for this purpose) and place another pin or tacking stitch at this 3in (8cm) point.

4. Count how many stitches lie between your two markers – this may mean including half stitches or even thirds, which will make all the difference to the final size. Divide by 3 to get your stitch tension. Then count up the rows between the top and bottom markers and divide by 3. In the swatch shown here there are 7 stitches and 8 rows.

Ideally you should treat the swatch the way it will be treated once it is part of the finished garment: wash it according to the guidelines, steam it, block it (see page 158) and do what you will be doing to the final item. If you do not, you might find it distorts and changes after washing and wearing. This is particularly true when you are using an open or elaborate lacy stitch.

1

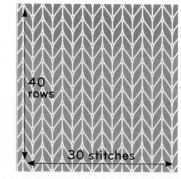

2

3

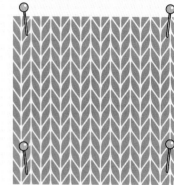

4

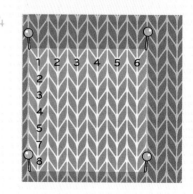

WHAT TO DO WITH YOUR TENSION (GAUGE) SWATCH

If your tension is the same as the original pattern, you know you are at least on the right track with your yarn choice.

If your tension is tighter (i.e. more stitches to the inch than the pattern recommends), knit up another square using needles a size larger. If it is looser (i.e. fewer stitches to the inch than recommended), try again using a smaller needle size. If you cannot match the original exactly, do not worry, you can adjust the pattern according to your own tension, but it is useful to get as close as possible.

Taking our 'Tea-Time Jumper' as an example, I knitted up a tension swatch in the main lacy stitch of the jumper. I knitted it over two pattern groups and three patterns high, which came to about 4in (10cm) square, to give me a fair idea of how the fabric would sit. I then blocked it out on an ironing board, placed my measuring markers and found that the stitch tension was the same as that in the pattern – this happens more often than you would think!

Two swatches for the 'Tea-Time Jumper', in mustard silk/wool mix and pink alpaca.

WHAT TO DO IF THERE IS NO TENSION (GAUGE) GUIDE

Some vintage patterns, particularly from the 1920s, do not give a tension guide but there are ways around this. If the pattern lists the measurements, find out the number of stitches at the widest part of the bust, then divide that by the bust measurement. For example, if the front measures 17in (42.5cm), and the number of stitches on the needle before you start decreasing for the armhole is 122, then you calculate as shown in equation A. Your stitch tension guideline will be 8 stitches = 1in (2.5cm).

If the pattern provides you with any other width measurements, perform a similar calculation using that number to back up your original conclusion – if the numbers match, you are good to go. If the length of the garment is referred to, you can then move on to the rows, using the same formula.

Pro tip

Do not cut corners on tension swatching: make sure your test square is knitted in the exact stitch. If you are planning to alter widths, swatch up the stitches of any areas affected by the alterations (i.e. rib, etc.).

A.

122 [number of stitches]

$\div$

17 [front width]

$=$

7 [stitches to 1in (2.5cm)]

SEE ALSO *Taking your measurements, page 30, Deconstruct to reconstruct, page 32, Finding yarn to suit your pattern, page 42*

WHAT TO DO IF YOU DO NOT KNOW THE MEASUREMENTS

Occasionally patterns do not list any measurements at all, so you have to assess the pattern picture and the instructions very closely and create your own guidelines. This does mean a bit more work, but if the pattern is a real beauty then you might feel it is worth the extra effort.

First of all, the pattern will probably give you needle sizes – as we will find out, these are a good clue to how thick the recommended yarn is. Have a close look at the pattern image – how does the garment drape? Does it look like a dense, close-together stitch using fine yarn, or does it have a delicate, lacy feel to it?

When in doubt, knit up as many swatches as you can until you feel comfortable that you have an approximation of the original garment's fabric. Once you think you are close, take a note of the tension and work out your width and length calculations from there, based on your own body measurements.

In the event of either of the above scenarios, do not forget to account for any negative ease (see 'Easy on the ease', page 31) that you think should be applied to the garment when you are coming up with your final calculations.

From the 1940s to the 1960s, knitting needles were often made in these lively colours.

Taking your measurements

An accurate map of your body measurements is essential before you start work on your garment. You might think you know your measurements, but your body can change shape over time – so it is useful to check them again each time you start a new project.

Which measurements to take

①	Bust	36in (90cm)	⑨	Back neck to waist	18½in (46.25cm)
②	Waist	30in (75cm)	⑩	Back neck to hip	23in (57.5cm)
③	Hips	38in (95cm)	⑪	Armhole depth	9in (22.5cm)
④	Neck to waist	16½in (41.25cm)	⑫	Arm length	23½in (58.75cm)
⑤	Shoulder to waist	18in (45cm)	⑬	Cuff	7½in (18.75cm)
⑥	Shoulder	5in (12.5cm)	⑭	Underarm length	19½in (48.75cm)
⑦	Neck	6in (15cm)	⑮	Upper arm circumference	12½in (31.25cm)
⑧	Back shoulder	16in (40cm)			

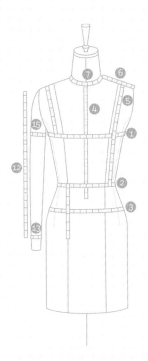

Pro tip

Some knitting books advise taking measurements from a piece of clothing that fits you well, but in this case I would advise against that. Modern garments have a different fit, which is largely down to the ease.

It helps if you have a friend to do this with you – it is not impossible on your own, but you might end up with readings that are not entirely accurate. Keep your underwear on, but do remove your outer clothing. As many vintage patterns use negative ease (see box below), you need your body measurements to be as accurate as possible. Using a dressmaker's (flexible) tape measure, take the following measurements:

Torso widths
1. *Bust* (fullest part of the bust)

2. *Waist* (narrowest part of the waist, approximately 1in (2.5cm) above the navel)

3. *Hips* (fullest part of the body)

Front measurements
4. *Neck to waist* (measured from the centre base of the neck)

5. *Shoulder to waist* (measured from base of neck at shoulder point to waist, over your bust)

6. *Shoulder* (from base of neck to tip of shoulder)

7. *Neck* (neck measurement)

Back measurements
8. *Back shoulder* width

9. *Back neck to waist*

10. *Back neck to hip* (or where your garment will end comfortably)

Arm
11. *Armhole depth* (top edge of shoulder to central underarm point)

12. *Arm length* (shoulder to wrist)

13. *Cuff* (wrist circumference)

14. *Underarm length* (from armpit to wrist)

15. *Upper arm circumference*

You will not necessarily use all these measurements in your calculations, but it is useful to have them to hand so you can compare the original garment measurements. I have included my measurements in the chart opposite as an example, which we will use to compare against the original size of the 'Tea-Time Jumper'..

Easy on the ease

'Ease' is the term used to describe the amount of space between your body and the garment. 'Negative ease', on the other hand, is where the garment is smaller than the wearer's actual measurements.

Ease will vary depending on the style of garment you are knitting and is something you will have to use your judgement for. The standard ease for modern garments is a comfortable 2 to 4in (5 to 10cm), but between the 1930s and 1950s,

when a tighter, more fitted look was favoured, garments tended to have a negative ease of 1 to 2in (2.5 to 5cm), i.e., garments were knitted 1 to 2in (2.5 to 5cm) smaller than the wearer's measurements.

You need to decide how much ease you are comfortable with versus the style of the original garment. Too much ease and you will lose the fitted vintage look, whereas too much negative ease might produce an uncomfortable garment.

I tend to steer away from too much negative ease, balancing a fitted look with something I will be comfortable wearing. The measurements I use in my reconstructed pattern planning reflect my measurements, giving a fit that is close to the skin with maybe up to ½in (1.25cm) ease, depending on the garment.

Do not forget, you will need to cater for more ease when knitting a cardigan to fit over other garments.

Deconstruct to reconstruct

In 'Finding & assessing your pattern', we looked at how the pattern is broken down into segments that guide you through making up the garment. In this section we will be examining that information in more detail to build an accurate picture of the original garment, so that you can create your own template to work from. Again, we will be using the 'Tea-Time Jumper' as an example.

PIECING TOGETHER
THE ORIGINAL PATTERN

One good way to break the pattern down is to draw up a table of statistics taken from the instructions. Have a look at the table opposite to see the details taken from the 'Tea-Time Jumper'.

There are gaps in our information: measurements such as the depth of the armhole and the length from armhole to hem would be useful here, as would a more accurate bust measurement – the broad range of 34 to 37in (85 to 92.5cm) clearly implies some stretching and ease – so by using your tension guide and reading closely through the pattern, you can make the assumptions about measurements given in the 'Missing details' table opposite.

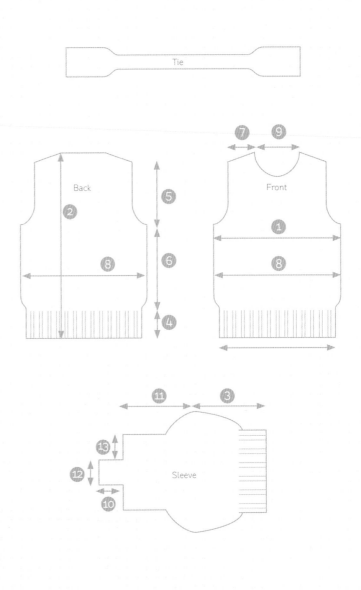

'Tea-Time Jumper' details

	Yarn	Golden Eagle Lustre Suede 3-ply
	Yarn quantity	7oz
	Needles	Nos. 10 & 12
	Tension (gauge)	7 stitches and 10 rows = 1in (2.5cm) over main pattern on No. 10 needles
(1)	Bust measurement	34 to 37in (85 to 92.5cm)
(2)	Length from back neck to lower edge	18in (45cm)
(3)	Sleeve down underarm	5in (12.5cm)
(4)	Waistband ribbing	4in (10cm)
	Stitch pattern group count	Groups of 12 sts + 2 extra over 10 rows

Missing details

(5)	Armhole depth (centre of underarm to shoulder)	67 rows	$6\frac{3}{4}$in (16.75cm)
(6)	Length from armhole to hem	70 rows + 4in (10cm) ribbing	11in (27.5cm)
(7)	Shoulder seam	30 sts	$4\frac{1}{4}$in (10.7cm)
(8)	Waist measurement	122 sts per side	$17\frac{5}{8}$in (43.5cm) × 2 = $34\frac{7}{8}$in (87.13cm)
(9)	Neck	38 sts	$5\frac{1}{2}$in (13.75cm)
(10)	Sleeve crown height	49 rows	5in (12.5cm)
(11)	Sleeve box height	30 rows	3in (7.5cm)
(12)	Sleeve box width	26 sts	$3\frac{1}{2}$in (9.25cm)
(13)	Sleeve box shoulder width	24 sts	$3\frac{1}{2}$in (9.25cm)

UNDERSTANDING THE CALCULATIONS

My task was made easier by the fact that each pattern group spans 10 rows, which just so happens to equal 1in (2.5cm) in the tension guide, so my calculations were made as follows:

- **Measurement 5:** I have worked out from the pattern that 67 rows are worked from the start of the armhole shaping to shoulder cast off, which equals 6¾in (16.75cm).

- **Measurement 6:** The instructions tell me to work 7 complete patterns until armhole shaping begins. According to the tension guide I know that equals 7in (17.5cm). I have added that to the 4in (10cm) ribbed waistband, and now know that from armhole to hem is 11in (27.5cm).

- **Measurement 7:** The shoulder seam measurements were calculated by looking at the instructions for the front. There are 122 stitches on the needle before the neck shaping begins; 10 stitches are cast off for the neckline. The neck-shaping decreases end with 30 stitches on the needle for each shoulder (see equation A).

- **Measurement 8:** After the waistband ribbing, the pattern increases the stitch count to 122 sts where it remains until the armhole shaping, making it the widest point at the bust. To find the measurement for this widest point, follow equation B. Of course that is just for one side; I have then doubled it to get the overall bust size.

- **Measurement 9:** For the neck: the number of stitches on the needle before you cast off for the neck and shoulders is 98. The shoulders end up with 30 stitches each, which leaves 38 stitches for the neckhole. Follow equation C to find this measurement.

- **Measurement 10:** The sleeve crown is worked over nearly five sets of patterns. We know that one pattern equals 10 rows and that 10 rows equals 1in (2.5cm), which means that 5in (12.5cm) is worked for the sleeve crown.

- **Measurement 11:** The length of the sleeve box is worked over three sets of patterns, which equals 30 rows. These 30 rows equal 3in (7.5cm).

- **Measurement 12:** The width of the sleeve box is worked over 26 sts. Using our tension guide, I divide 26 by 7 to get a rough width of 3½in (9.25cm).

- **Measurement 13:** The 'shoulders' of the sleeve crown are created by casting off 24 sts. Dividing our tension of 7 by 24 gives us roughly 3½in (9.25cm).

A.

30 sts [shoulder stitches on needle]
$$\div$$
7 [stitch tension]
$$=$$
4¼in (10.7cm)

B.

122 sts [stitches at widest point]
$$\div$$
7 [stitch tension]
$$=$$
17⅜in (44.1cm)

C.

38 sts [neckhole stitches]
$$\div$$
7 [stitch tension]
$$=$$
5½in (13.75cm) [rounded up]

The classic Victory jumper first appeared in the popular UK magazine *Home Notes* in June 1945, designed to celebrate the end of WWII. It is available on the Victoria & Albert Museum website (see 'Useful resources', page 160).

COMPARING MEASUREMENTS

Doing those calculations gives you an essential starting point. Even if you quickly glance over the pattern at the assessment stage and think that the measurements given will match your own, these more accurate details give you an idea of the amount of ease intended. Although the cover image shows the jumper has a very slight blouson effect, that bust size of 35 to 37in (85 to 92.5cm) mentioned at the beginning of the pattern compared to our own stitch/measurement calculation of 34⅞in (87.13cm) says we are running into negative ease.

You now know exactly what you are dealing with and can compare the garment size with the table of your own measurements that you took in the previous section. You can make up a table by taking your own measurements, comparing them with that of the garment and calculating the changes you will need to make – see the table below, which uses my measurements and that of the 'Tea-Time Jumper'.

Comparative measurements

Body	My body measurements	Original measurements	Difference
Bust	36in (90cm)	34⅞in (87.13cm)	1⅛in (2.8cm)
Waist	30in (75cm)	27in (67.5cm)	3in (7.5cm)
Hips	38in (95cm)	–	–
Shoulder to waist	18in (45cm)	18in (45cm)	–
Shoulder	5in (12.5cm)	5½in (13.75cm)	½in (1cm)
Neck	6in (15cm)	4¼in (10.7cm)	¾in (1.8cm)
Back shoulder	15in (40cm)	14in (35cm)	1in (2.5cm)
Back neck to waist	18½in (46.25cm)	18in (45cm)	½in (1cm)
Armhole depth	8½in (21.25cm)	6¾in (16.75cm)	1¾in (4.5cm)
Arm length	23½in (58.75cm)	–	–
Cuff	7½in (18.75cm)	–	–
Underarm length	5in (12.5cm)	5in (12.5cm)	–
Upper arm circumference	14in (35cm)	14in (35cm)	–

SKETCHING OR CHARTING OUT THE DESIGN

This useful table of measurements might be enough for you, but I also find it handy to translate them into a sketch or chart, sometimes both. Some of the original patterns conveniently provide a ready-made sketch (the 'Tea-Time Jumper' does), but do not count on it!

My own notebooks are no works of art, but the main thing is that I am able to build up an accurate picture of my past projects to remember how I approached them. I make as many notes as I can so I do not forget the rationale behind some of my decisions. Knitter's graph paper will come in very handy for this, for life-size or scaled-down models. It is also essential when you are plotting out Fair Isle or stitch patterns (see page 140).

You can create a full-size version of the original pattern using knitter's graph paper or dressmaker's spot-and-cross paper, using the measurements above. This can then be reused to superimpose your measurements. You can take this as a base for your revised pattern, translating the shaping into knitted fabric by using your tension calculations.

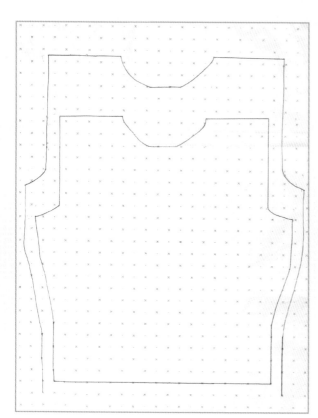

The original 'Tea-Time Jumper' measurements plotted out in blue on spot-and-cross paper, with our revised measurements marked in red.

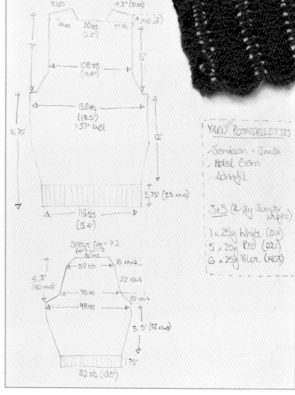

My sketchbook page for the Victory jumper (page 35) includes original measurements plotted out, yarn options and a tension swatch.

CREATE A TOILE

If you are feeling particularly dedicated, are handy with a sewing machine and want to go one step further to ensure a more accurate fit, you might even decide to make up a toile, which is a mocked-up model of the garment, or prototype.

If you think the original might fit but you want to make absolutely sure, you could create a toile at this deconstruction stage, but generally it is something you will want to do when you are planning your revised version.

This might not be something you want (or have the time) to repeat on every project, but it is an interesting procedure that helps to demystify the garment and gives you a more definitive map to guide the way.

If you were making a toile for a dressmaking project you would probably use calico or a similar fabric, but knitted fabric stretches and eases, so calico would be too rigid for your purposes – you need something with a drape and texture all of its own, so it is best to go for something like jersey to re-create the effect.

SEE ALSO *Tension & tension swatching, page 26, Taking your measurements, page 30*

TOILE METHOD

For this method you will need the following:

- Dressmaker's spot-and-cross paper or large sheets of paper
- Pencil
- Set square
- Rigid ruler
- 2¼ yards (2m) jersey fabric

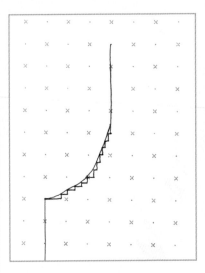

1. Start with a point of your garment shape which you will use as your anchor mark (say the bottom left of the waistband) and measure out the longest and widest points, creating marks on the paper as you go.

2. Next you need to plot out the shaping: since we are dealing with a pre-written pattern you can see where increases and decreases are made in the garment and transfer them to your own toile pattern accordingly. Your row tension guidelines will come in handy here too: for example, if the instructions tell you to decrease at

each end of every following alternate row over 10 rows and your tension guideline is 10 rows to the inch, you know those decreases will be made over 1in (2.5cm) and will plot that out on the toile accordingly.

3. To join the dots you will need to create curves, particularly where the sleeves are concerned. Since we are working with graph paper we are creating an angular shape rather than a curved one, but as the instructions will make it clear where shaping is made, it should be clear where you need to give the toile some curves (see illustration left: original pattern marks are in blue, added curves are in red).

4. Knitted garments do not give you a seam allowance, but you will need one for the toile, so add an extra ½in (or 1cm) all round.

5. Cut out your pattern (including the seam allowance) and pin it to your fabric, taking care not to stretch it as you do so.

6. Cut out the fabric and remove the pattern.

7. Make up the toile as you would do the knitted garment: with right sides together, pin and sew the shoulder and side seams, then pin and sew the sleeves into place.

8. Press the seams open, turn the garment right side out and you are done.

A toile for the 'Tea-Time Jumper', made up using the revised measurements, to check for fit.

Background to vintage yarns

One of the biggest hurdles to knitting vintage patterns is wading through the mystery surrounding the yarns used, particularly when they give no information about content or yardage. Throw into the mix the confusion of differing international yarn terms and it is enough to put anyone off. So here is a brief background to some of the yarns you might come across.

VINTAGE YARNS PRE-1950s

We are so familiar with today's yarn terms that curious names such as Patons Fair Isle Fingering, Golden Eagle 'Lustre Suede' and Bucilla French Zephyr might as well be written in Latin, but despite all the unfamiliar brands there is one thing you can be pretty sure of: with the exception of artificial silk or rayon, which entered the scene in the 1930s, pre-1950 none of them will have contained any synthetics, mixed or pure. That does not mean to say that the wools themselves were not mixed, textured or flecked: cotton and bouclé were popular, for example, particularly during the 1930s.

In 1937, one of the best-known knitting gurus, Mary Thomas, made a list of the yarn varieties then available: 'Wool Yarns, Fancy Yarns, Irregular Twisting (i.e. Bouclé), Mixtures, Flecked Yarns, Crepe Yarns' and mentions cotton, suede, silk, rayon, linen, jute and mercerised yarns besides angora, astrakhan, camel hair and cashmere.

As a rule of thumb, yarns pre-1950s tended to be slightly thicker if anything than their modern-day equivalents so often you will find a fine 4-ply yarn nowadays will knit to a similar tension as a vintage 3-ply. But you should never assume this to be the case – as ever, your tension swatch will guide you.

Scotch Wool proudly displayed their Greenock factory and retail outlets on the back of their patterns from the 1920s to the 1940s – a nod to their heritage.

SEE ALSO Finding yarn to suit your pattern, page 42, Calculating yardage & weight, page 48

POST-WAR YARNS

Lastex (or elastic) thread had entered the market by the mid-1930s but was not being used in knitting, and WWII put a halt to any further developments. Post-war was a different story – one of the by-products of the developments in space travel was polyester. Pure wool was still widely used, though some, labelled 'shrink resist', was now treated chemically or mechanically to provide extra endurance and prevent felting. Yarns used from the late 1950s onwards would be more familiar to us now, and some of the names have survived.

If you are knitting from a pattern from the mid-1960s onwards, you should have very little problem identifying an appropriate yarn: 4-ply, DK and bulky yarns were all far more common. Yarn names also tended to give more of a hint about their content, and you are safe in the knowledge that a synthetic mix will be appropriate. Some of the ranges are still being manufactured today, or at least they were within living memory and can be traced through their present brand owners.

NEXT STEPS

To demystify the process of choosing a yarn, in the next sections we will look at vintage weights versus modern, how to calculate yardage and weight, and how to understand the different UK and US yarn classifications.

Begin by paying particular attention to the pattern, teasing out clues from your pattern image, tension and yard description, and start to experiment with tension swatches until you end up with something you are happy with. Easy!

Vintage yarn adverts often provide information about the original yarn. This 1950s example gives details about the yarn mix.

Finding yarn to suit your pattern

This is one of the conundrums most likely to deter a knitter from attempting an old pattern. Do not become too overwhelmed by the vintage brand names and descriptions. Your pattern will give you more clues than may be immediately apparent – prepare to make some assumptions, experiment and enjoy your final decision!

HOW TO IDENTIFY THE ORIGINAL YARN

Carefully reading the yarn description, needle size and tension information and looking at the pattern image and description will give you more knowledge than you might think.

Yarn description

This will give you your first (and most obvious) clue to the original yarn. Let us take the yarn used in our 'Tea-Time Jumper' as an example. We are told that it is Golden Eagle 'Lustre Suede' 3-ply. I know nothing about this yarn so I am going to make a couple of big leaps of assumption here. The name 'Lustre Suede' suggests two things to me: softness and a slight sheen, which gets me thinking of silk.

The term 3-ply? Well, that has helpfully narrowed it down even more. So for now I am thinking about a 3-ply or sock-weight yarn in silk or silk mix.

Needles & tension (gauge)

These are vital clues – you will find that the more vintage patterns you look at and knit from, the more you will get to know what kind of thickness of yarn you are looking for from these simple bits of information.

In this instance the pattern tells me that the needle requirements are one pair each of Nos. 10 and 12, so if the yarn description had not already spelt it out, I would know from this that I would need a fine yarn to knit on these fine needles.

The tension guidelines tell me that 1in (2.5cm) = 7 stitches and 10 rows, again an indication that this is a fine yarn (see 'Yarn charts', page 54).

Although knitted to the same tension, the silk/wool mix yarn (top) and the alpaca yarn make two very different fabrics, which affects the drape and shape of the garment.

Pattern image & description

Both fairly obvious clues, they reveal more than you might think. As we saw earlier, there is a clue in the description: yes, the lacy stitch lends it a delicate air, but it has a strength that gives it warmth too. I am now looking for a wool/silk mix.

So, our garment is knitted in a fairly open lace stitch, obviously knitted to a fine tension on a fine yarn. But look closer and you will see that the stitch has a good, clear definition to it – the yarn clearly has some substance to give it that kind of stitch outline, so you are not dealing with an incredibly delicate yarn. Another clue can be found in the sleeves with those wonderful box heads – some structure is needed to keep them upright.

You will need to consider what kind of yarn will result in the 'drape' you see on the original garment. Drape is the term used to refer to how the garment hangs: is your fabric stiff and unyielding or does it flow (i.e. if you place it over your hand does it drape and hang, or does it keep its shape and remain fairly rigid?)

Generally when you are knitting on fine needles you will get a fairly dense fabric, which is why fine yarn is called for – the finer and softer the yarn, the more relaxed the drape. You can see the difference in the two examples of the 'Tea-Time Jumper' – one knitted in a silk/wool mix, one in alpaca, both knitted from an identical pattern and with the same tension (see photos left). The sleeves of the pink alpaca jumper do not quite give the firm structure of the original.

The original pattern for the Bestway 'Tea-Time Jumper'.

The updated version knitted in pink alpaca. Note the softer structure of the box-top sleeves and the stitch definition.

CHOOSING A YARN TO MATCH

From my pattern assessments, I now know I am looking for a 3-ply silk/wool mix equivalent. I know the pattern is from the UK (British needle sizes and the fact that Bestway were a British firm give that away) from the 1940s, although possibly not from the WWII era itself judging by the style and materials: I cannot imagine a silk-mix yarn being recommended at the height of the restrictions, and the lacy stitch does seem a little frivolous for the practical war days, so I am looking for a colour to suit the post-war era.

The black-and-white image flattens everything out so even mid-shades can look a stark white, and there is no colour guidance in the instructions, so after changing my mind two or three times (pale blue was in the running for a while) and a couple of tension swatches later I eventually settled on a classic 1940s mustard yellow.

Pro tip

If you do not know the yarn, do a quick internet search just in case someone has some information about it and then ask around on some forums – this might spark an interest and increases the chances of information being spread.

Original yarns from the 1950s.

BE PREPARED TO COMPROMISE AND EXPERIMENT

From your deductions and colour choices you may now have narrowed your selection down to a 3-ply merino/silk/wool mix in a particular shade of faded aqua only to find that it either does not exist or is not available in your country. You might have to expand your search to cut out one of the fibre mixes, or try a different colour, or change yarn weights slightly and experiment with tension swatches in a 4-ply instead.

The reason I went from a pale blue to a mustard yellow was that I could not find the colour I had in my mind. I experimented with three or four different shades and yarns before I thought I was getting close to my final choice. I had bought a sample of the yellow purely because I liked the colour and had it in mind for another project – happy coincidence that three or four swatches later the yellow just felt right.

The vibrancy of original yarns can be surprising if you are used to black-and-white images.

THICKNESS

Try not to stray too far from the original weight and tension – using a DK where a 3-ply is called for will produce a bulkier item, which will detract from that fine fabric finish that the lighter yarns produce, no matter how much tension and pattern adjustment you apply.

But it can be easy to get hooked up and caught out on the different ply terms, particularly for UK patterns. As those redoubtable knitting writers from the 1940s, Jane Kostner and Margaret Murray, point out, 'a ply can be of any number of strands or counts so that a thick 2-ply can be thicker than some 3-ply yarns'.

My choice of yarn (a good-quality 30 per cent silk/70 per cent wool mix) is a 4-ply equivalent. Given that vintage yarns were slightly thicker, I do not have too much of a problem with this. I think it is a shave bulkier than the original yarn, but the tension is identical to that given in the pattern and the drape is still fluid.

I also considered using an alpaca yarn, which would at least give the desired softness if not the 'lustre'. Swatching it, the tension was also identical to the pattern so I knew I was on the right track, but the stitch definition would not be so sharp and it would be a lighter, more delicate fabric. It would still make a beautiful jumper if not slightly different from that shown in the pattern image, so I also knitted the jumper in alpaca to illustrate how your yarn choice can alter the final outcome of your garment. The photo here shows the different effects. The pink jumper was knitted in the softer alpaca, and the mustard in the silk/wool mix.

Our two 'Tea-Time Jumpers' brought to life after nearly seventy years.

NATURAL OR SYNTHETIC?

Up to now we have been talking about 100 per cent wool or natural fibres, which are more historically accurate. While these yarns can be surprisingly economical, you may find yourself straying into expensive territory when it comes to more exotic mixes. Would it be easier to source from a local shop that maybe does not have the best selection?

Why not experiment with a synthetic mix? My very first vintage garment was knitted from a 1954 *Vogue Knitting* book using a white baby-knit 3-ply that was a 50/50 wool/

nylon mix: very cheap and very easy to knit with. Even though I knew it was not a close match to the original material it still looked like a vintage blouse, so I am not going to knock it.

It could be an economical, quick and easy way to get you on the road to vintage knitting experimentation, and you may even catch yourself eyeing up a softer or more natural yarn for your next project, or craving something a little closer to the original – whatever you choose, experimentation is the way forwards.

Pro tip

One evening, why not pour yourself a glass of something nice and prepare for some wonderful online searching? I have found great wool from the UK, the USA, Denmark, Australia, Iceland, and Sweden.

WHERE TO FIND SUITABLE YARNS

When I first started knitting from vintage patterns, the only fine yarns that seemed to be available to me existed in the world of baby knits in appropriately sugary colours, and mostly consisted of a synthetic mix.

Since then the internet has offered a new world of choice and that, combined with a resurgence of interest in all things vintage, means that different colours and thicknesses are available again. The rise in popularity of sock knitting

has also had its part to play in the demand for finer yarns, and that seems to have kick-started a small fine-yarn revolution.

Of course, vintage patterns do not only use fine yarns: you may find the occasional reference to 8-ply, or advice to use two strands of 4-ply, in which case you may assume that good old worsted or DK is called for. You will find a chart in the next section that cross-references specific territorial yarn terms

and their international equivalents (see page 54).

It is up to you where you buy your yarn. You may have a favourite local yarn shop with a great range to experiment with, and you may prefer to be environmentally friendly by buying from your own country. You will find a list of suppliers in 'Useful resources' (see page 160).

SEE ALSO *Tension & tension swatching, page 26, Colours, page 50*

A late 1930s jumper pattern using a popular (although yarn-hungry) bobble stitch.

Calculating yardage & weight

For the first couple of vintage projects I knitted up, I tried guessing the amount I needed – and both times I wildly over-estimated. This can become a rather expensive exercise, and equally frustrating if you under-estimate and cannot get hold of the same yarn dye lot as you started out with.

UNRAVELLING YOUR TENSION SWATCH

Calculating yardage is not an exact science, but there is a simple method you can use to get you in the ball-park and nail down a more accurate guesstimate.

Follow these easy steps to estimate the amount you will need.

1. Knit up a swatch with the yarn you want to use for your pattern in the garment's main stitch and measure the width and height.

2. Unravel the swatch (make sure you snip off any long ends) and measure the length of yarn.

3. Multiply the swatch width and height to calculate the total square inches.

4. Divide the total square inches by the amount of yarn you used.

For the 'Tea-Time Jumper' I knitted up a swatch measuring 4in (10cm) square. When I unravelled the yarn it measured 17¾ yards (16.2m). I multiplied the measurements of my swatch to estimate the coverage area of the garment, then divided this by the amount of yarn I had used. (Note: as vintage patterns are worked in inches, I will base my calculations on imperial measurements.) My swatch measured 4 × 4in and I used 17¾ yards of yarn for this. To work out how much yarn I needed per square inch, I calculated as shown in equation A.

So now you know how many yards/metres per square inch needed. You then need to calculate the overall area of the fabric used, as follows.

1. Block-sketch your pattern using a vertical rectangle for the body and a smaller block for the sleeve.

2. Take the longest and widest measurements that you calculated during your 'Deconstruct to reconstruct' phase and apply them to your blocks. Remember, this is going to be a rough guide and, if anything, it is best to have some yarn left over.

3. Multiply the length and width of each block and add them all up to get the total square inches of your garment (do not forget to double them if you only drew one block for one side and one sleeve).

4. Multiply the total square inches by the yarn length per square inch to give the total amount of yarn required (equation B).

5. Do not forget to add in extra amounts for details such as neck-ties, belts, intricate cuffs, etc. When in doubt, always round up.

The yarn I used came in 221-yard skeins, so I divided the total amount of yarn required by the skein length as shown in equation C.

I added 20 per cent to cover any unforeseen inaccuracies (the main stitch the garment is knitted in can also have an effect on the amount of yarn you use) and bought seven skeins of yarn for my pattern. The estimate took me very close: I used 6½ skeins for the whole garment.

SEE ALSO *Tension and tension swatching, page 26, Deconstruct to reconstruct, page 32*

A.

16 [size of swatch]

÷

17.71 [yarn used]

=

0.91 yards

B.

1,386 [total square inches]

×

0.91 [yds per square inch]

=

1,261 [total amount
of yarn yds required]

C.

1,261 [garment coverage
in square inches]

÷

221 yds [skein length]

=

5.7 [skeins]

Original yarns were sold according
to weight.

THE IMPORTANCE OF TENSION SWATCHES

I like to hang on to my tension swatches for future reference, so I usually knit up two (one to keep, one to unravel for yarn estimation).

You might want to knit up swatches using the different stitches used in your garment and calculate the square area of each accordingly – you will be surprised how much the yarn requirements can vary depending on the stitch pattern, especially with yarn-hungry ones such as cable patterns.

Pro tip

Keep details in your notebook of how much yarn you estimated versus how much yarn you used, how you calculated it, and your tension swatch – the more details you keep, the easier it will be to work out future adaptations.

Colours

The right colour can make or break your vintage knitwear – use the wrong shade of green and you could update your garment to the extent that it looks like a modern pattern. This is fine if that is your intent, but if you want to be more faithful to your vintage look, then read on.

VINTAGE COLOURS

We are so used to seeing our vintage served to us in black and white that it is easy to disregard the original colour palettes, or to unconsciously mark them down to more neutral or natural shades. Have a look through some of the wonderful mid- to late 1930s patterns or peer a little more closely at the suggested yarn colours in the 'Materials' sections and you will discover a lively world of colour exploding into existence.

We have a choice to make: are we going for the original colours, or are we basing our decision on an attempt to make a new garment look old? Unknowingly, the colours we select for our vintage projects can come down to the choice between our perception of a vintage look from today's viewpoint versus actual colours used during the period we are knitting from.

Pro tip

Give your colour scheme a good bit of consideration before you leap into a project, and decide what result you are aiming to achieve.

You can see from the black-and-white image how difficult it is to assess the vintage colours. The 1930s palette in particular could be brighter than you might think.

The vivid green pictured in this late 1940s pattern suggests the more exuberant colour range that returned after WW II restrictions were lifted.

Bold contrast stripes were a common feature in the 1950s. Here they are used to enhance the unusual sleeve design.

COLOURS IN THE 1920s & 1930s

During WWI, availability of dyes diminished, which led to a less saturated palette that was to extend into much of the 1920s. Almost as if to deny hints of femininity, 1920s fashions steered clear of colour and tended towards neutral, bland shades with the odd flashes of jade green, cerise and red. Sometimes different shades of blue were seen in a striped or chevron pattern, which reflected the Art Deco trend.

Taking the lead from Paris as ever, the combination of red, white and blue recurred through the late 1920s and 1930s, and gave the garments they trimmed or decorated a French nautical air.

Accents & contrasts

Another persistent colour scheme throughout the 1930s was the use of a plain black background to show up highlights of a more vivid colour, and white accents were popular in the form of crocheted collars and cuffs. A *Stitchcraft* magazine from December 1937 states, 'Black is the wool-colour-of-the-moment', and goes on to describe an 'afternoon-cum-cocktail frock (black again) with a yellow-lined sash'.

A front cover from a 1937 *Woman's Own* shows a light pink bodice with contrasting deep pink (almost burgundy) collar, belt and welts.

Avant-garde fashion designer Elsa Schiaparelli was a huge advocate of sky-blue and what we now know as shocking pink, which became something of a trademark colour for her, while Parisian couturier Jean Patou favoured citron yellow.

This Schiaparelli-endorsed yarn advertisement from 1934 shows a wonderful pistachio green.

The soft, summery blue in this pattern from 1933 complements the flowing cape sleeves and airy drape.

In another pattern from 1933, green and black are used as a vivid contrast for a bolder look.

COLOURS IN THE 1940s

The early 1940s was a strange time for colour, which was subject to the restrictions and rationing of the time along with everything else. A limited spectrum reduced to drab khaki greens, navy blues, browns and mustard yellows was common. Greys, browns and Air Force blues were the other widely available colours, but there were ways to make a plain knit more colourful.

In *Practical Knitting Illustrated*, published in 1940, prolific hand-knit stalwarts Jane Koster and Margaret Murray discuss how to brighten up the more limited palette that was already creeping in. They refer to a 'women's classic jersey, made in navy blue with white tippings at neck, sleeves and welt edges'.

A section on colour stripes suggests, 'Greys, fawns and heather mixtures are extremely pleasing'. They go on to recommend, 'a grey cardigan with scarlet welts, sleeves knitted in a different colour, or contrasting backs and fronts'.

Being inventive

Unravelling old knits could provide some brightness: a jumper from an early 1940s *Needlework Illustrated* uses lengths of ribbon threaded through drop-stitch bands. There follows a pattern for a cardigan with a dark background 'featuring slimming stripes knitted with odds and ends of wool. The model cardigan was made in navy blue and the stripes were in rose, Wedgwood [blue], grey, lemon and green.'

Another pattern from this magazine suggests you use 'any pretty colour, or a gay one such as scarlet which looks wonderful with both light and dark skirts'.

The limits imposed by the war took a while to disappear. An issue of *Woman's Weekly* from January 1946 sees a return to colour suggestions, but they were still very much generic: a pattern for a Fair Isle lists red, brown, blue, green and yellow instead of the more descriptive colours used in patterns from later on in the decade.

You will often find unusual colour combinations that you have otherwise avoided for fear of clashing.

A wonderful deep green jacket is broken up with chevron pockets in a darker shade of green and white.

Blue is a perennial favourite and a safe bet if you are unsure which colour to use for a 1940s-vintage project, particularly Air Force blue.

COLOURS IN THE 1950s & 1960s

The 1950s saw pastels and sherbet tones providing a refreshing, rejuvenating deliverance from subdued wartime colours. Fabric, yarn and dyes were back in production, but black and white were as fashionable as ever, particularly in eveningwear.

Later in the decade stronger, more vibrant colours started to emerge, offset by neutral beiges, creams and blacks. The Italian couture industry was starting to rival French dominance and making its influence felt firmly in the turquoises, oranges and hot pinks that would carry on into the 1960s, championed by Italian designers such as Emilio Pucci and Simonetta Visconti.

The 1960s was the most colourful decade of the century: geometric designs were accentuated by bright primary colours. Art was allied to fashion in a way Elsa Schiaparelli had only hinted at, and influence was taken from artists such as Mondrian. The more contemporary influence of Andy Warhol resulted in the emergence of brighter, bolder, neon colours.

Thanks to the continuing influence of the Italian design movement, oranges were matched with clashing pinks, yellows and reds in psychedelic combinations, designed to push fashion forwards into realms it had never entered before.

These bright pastel stripes are typical of the fresh use of colour in the 1950s.

The deep lilac and beaded decoration in this 1950s evening jumper hints at the opulence that post-war designers revelled in.

Here we see the same design, reissued later in the decade, in a vivid pink.

Yarn charts

INTERNATIONAL YARN CONVERSION

When you are looking at ways of determining what is available and appropriate for your pattern, familiarise yourself with common yarn terminology using the chart below, which will give you a better idea of specific yarn terms and their international equivalents.

This is a rough guide; it can vary slightly depending on your yarn and tension, so as ever, it is best to experiment. Please check the needle conversion chart on page 163 for equivalents to the suggested needle sizes.

The opportunities the internet now offers mean that the different territorial terms are becoming more familiar to knitters, but unless there is a standard international agreement any time soon, you will need to keep referring to your conversion chart.

Yarn equivalents

Standard yarn weight	USA	UK	Australia	Suggested needle	WPI
0 or Lace	Laceweight or Cobweb	1-ply	1-ply	1.5–2.25mm	18+ wpi
1 or w4 or Medium	Fingering	2-ply	2-ply	2.25–3mm	16 wpi
5 or Bulky	Sock (or Light Fingering)	3-ply	3-ply	2.25–3.25mm	14 wpi
6 or Super Bulky	Sport	4-ply	4-ply	3.25–3.75mm	12 wpi
	DK/Light Worsted	DK	8-ply	3.75–4.5mm	11 wpi
	Worsted	Aran	10-ply	4.5–5.5mm	9 wpi
	Bulky	Chunky	12-ply	5.5–8mm	7 wpi
	Super Bulky	Super Chunky	14-ply	8mm+	5-6 wpi

WRAPPING METHOD GUIDE

In this method (also referred to as WPI), you wrap the yarn around a ruler or piece of evenly cut card and measure the number of wraps per inch (2.5cm). Make sure the yarn is wrapped so that it lies flat and even without any gaps, and try not to wrap it too loose or too tight, then take your measurement at the centre of the sample.

The table opposite gives you a rough guideline to refer to.

All kinds of modern yarns are suitable for use when you are adapting a vintage pattern. Compare the yarn conversion chart to the suggested needles on the belly band if you are unsure about suitability.

3. ADJUSTING VINTAGE SIZES

Adjusting widths

This is one of the most likely adjustments you will be faced with. Once you have taken your measurements and established as many dimensions as you can from the pattern, you will have a pretty good idea of where you will need to make the width adjustments.

WHERE TO START

The bust is the most obvious and crucial place to start as it is usually the widest part of the piece, but do not ignore the hips and waist. I once knitted a garment using the original pattern instructions for a 36in (90cm) bust, and the ribbed hemline over my waist and hips was far too tight – a lesson to work out my own measurements versus the pattern's, and to swatch each part of the garment depending on the different stitch patterns.

As we have seen, the average bust measurement in patterns from the 1930s to 1940s ranged from 32 to 34in (80 to 85cm), minus a bit of negative ease, with the occasional 36 to 38in (90 to 95cm) anomaly for the 'older woman' or 38 to 40in (95 to 100cm) for the 'fuller figure'. These became more common in the 1950s.

Start with a quick sketch in your knitting notebook. You may have already compared your own measurements to those in the original pattern in the 'Deconstruct to reconstruct' phase, so you will know which adjustments you are dealing with and where.

Widening the torso is not as simple as it sounds. If you add a few stitches to the main body, what do you do with them when you get to the armhole shaping? Or the shoulders? Let us break our width adjustments down into logical sections.

WIDENING THE TORSO/BUST

I often find that the bust-width adjustment can be used as a guide for the torso and hip widths – sometimes if you size the bust width up, the rest of the garment size will follow proportionally. Bear in mind that any width adjustments will be calculated using your tension as a guide (see page 24).

For example, if you are knitting from a pattern using a 34in (85cm) bust measurement (which works out to 33in [82.5cm] with a –1in [2.5cm] negative ease) and want to size up to a 36in bust with no ease, you are looking at a 3in (7.5cm) width increase. Say your tension is 7 stitches to the inch, you perform the calculation in equation A.

I round up by one stitch and cast (bind) on an extra 11 stitches for each side. The reason for rounding up is to make the number divisible by 2. When you are calculating how many stitches to cast on, always look ahead to the rest of the pattern and make sure you end up with the correct number of stitches to accommodate stitch or Fair Isle patterns.

Darts used for shaping (particularly horizontal ones) are pretty rare in vintage patterns although they did make more of an appearance in the 1950s. It is possible to work a couple of darts into your garment if you feel they are absolutely necessary and you are facing a dramatic difference between the bust width and the rest of the body.

A.

3in (7.5cm) [width increase]

×

7 sts [stitch tension]

=

21 sts

WIDENING THE HIPS

A typical jumper body will be made in the following stages:

- Start off by casting on the required number of stitches with a pair of needles that are a size or two finer than those used for the main body.

- Knit in a rib stitch for 3in (7.5cm) or 4in (10cm).

- Change to a larger needle and at the same time increase a certain number of stitches immediately (common in a blouson-style top), or begin to increase gradually either side of the garment towards the bust.

How to assess a ribbed hemline

If the hip measurements need adjusting and your garment starts with a ribbed hemline, swatch yourself a bit of rib using the appropriate yarn and needles. Of course the elasticity of the rib stitch gives you a fair bit of flexibility, but you need to be realistic about how far the rib will stretch. Not enough stretch and it will appear too loose, too much and it will appear strained and tight.

A good time-saving trick for assessing your ribbed hemline is to knit the given length of ribbing, then at the final row thread a piece of contrasting yarn through each stitch while they are still on the needle. Cast off loosely, and then measure your waistband while it is slightly stretched.

If you feel it is not wide enough then unravel and start again, recalculating the amount of stitches you cast on with. If you are happy with it, unravel the cast-off row, then pick up the stitches from the contrast thread and continue with your knitting.

What if your hips are wider than your bust?

You may find that your hips are the widest part of your body, in which case you will need to start off with more stitches than you will end up with at the bust.

In order to get to this point you will need to work a gradual decrease throughout the body until you get to your desired bust width before armhole shaping. This would be better implemented by decreasing stitches gradually at either side as your body narrows towards the bust, making sure that the width at the waist is accounted for.

Pro tip

A toile will help you to be more certain that the garment will fit, and exactly where to make the adjustments. It will also give you a clearer picture of the knock-on effects on the rest of your garment.

WIDENING THE WAIST

Many vintage patterns have a ribbed section at the waist to emphasise the shaping, or shape the waist using decreases and increases at both sides. When you come across such a pattern, it would be nice to assume that any adjustments you have calculated for the general width of the jumper would be proportionally taken into account at the waist too – but do not bet on it. If you are unsure, refer to your swatch or knit another one in the stitch used at the waist and check that the measurements tally with your body's own.

If you find yourself needing more width at the waist ribbing, consider adding it in at the cast-on stage. Alternatively you could add more stitches into any existing increases made at the end of the ribbed hemline, or a more gradual increase to either side of the garment in the build-up to the waist.

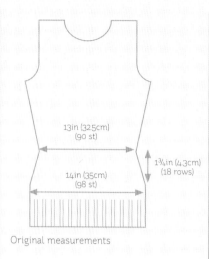

13in (32.5cm)
(90 st)

1¾in (4.3cm)
(18 rows)

14in (35cm)
(98 st)

Original measurements

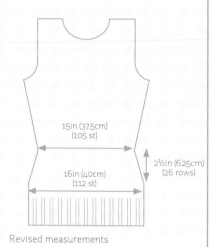

15in (37.5cm)
(105 st)

2½in (6.25cm)
(26 rows)

16in (40cm)
(112 st)

Revised measurements

NARROWING YOUR GARMENT

The calculations for narrowing your garment are, as you would expect, similar to the widening adjustments but in reverse. As ever, create swatches for each stitch used and re-calculate stitch amounts where necessary.

SUMMARY

Let us recap the width adjustments I made to the 'Tea-Time Jumper'.

- I calculated that I would need 18in (45cm) at the bust for each side and was happy with zero ease.

- I swatched my ribbed waistline and was happy that the results would produce a rib that, when stretched slightly, would fit my waist and hips, so I sized my pattern according to the new bust width.

- In this instance that meant adding 7 extra stitches to the cast-on amount, which also took into consideration the lacy stitch pattern (worked over groups of 12 stitches).

So you have made the adjustments to the main body of your garment up to the armhole shaping – now you will have to adapt the measurements to make sure they fit your shoulders.

SEE ALSO Taking your measurements, page 30, Adjusting armholes & sleeves, page 64, Adjusting shoulders, page 76, Working with Fair Isles & stitch patterns, page 82, Darts, page 104

Mocking up a toile is a great way to check that your measurements will work for your figure.

Adjusting lengths

If you are knitting from a vintage pattern, you may need to alter the length of your jumper or dress torso. The classic knitting pattern catered for torsos that were shorter and more narrow during the mid-twentieth century, skirt and trouser waistbands were worn higher, and undergarments tighter. The length from underarm to shoulder may also be a little tight – another result of smaller busts and narrower torsos.

LENGTHENING THE TORSO

This is a fairly common adjustment, and one of the easiest to make, but there are knock-on effects that you need to take into account.

Yarn shortages from the WWII era meant every row mattered and so knitted jumpers became shorter. During the 1930s to 1940s, the average length of a jumper from hem to shoulder seems to hover around the 18 to 19in (45 to 47.5cm) mark, which is at least 3in (7.5cm) too short for my twenty-first-century figure.

As the fashion during the 1920s was for a longer, more tubular appearance you might find you do not have to lengthen jumpers from this period, but where later patterns are concerned you may decide a bit of extra length would be a good thing without detracting from the original look.

At times it will not be immediately apparent what length is knitted in each section: for example, where a stitch pattern is used the instructions might read 'Repeat 10 patterns'. This is where your tension guide will come in handy: you can use it to work out how many patterns are knitted to the inch and calculate the original length accordingly.

This 1940s design was made using the original length measurements. You can see how a shorter torso and contrast ribbed waist welt was used to emphasise the waist.

DECIDING WHERE TO ADD LENGTH

Once you have worked out how the length of the original garment corresponds to your own measurements, you will get a better idea of where the length needs to be applied: for example, you might decide that you need to spread your extra inches over the garment rather than in just one place (an extra 1in [2.5cm] to the armholes and 2in [5cm] to the torso, for example). Where the pattern includes waist shaping, you might want to add 2in (5cm) below the waist and 1in (2.5cm) above.

Your decision will also be affected by the style and dimensions of the pattern. Consider the style of the pattern first and ask yourself a few questions:

- Where is the waistline intended to fall?

- Is there waist shaping to take into consideration?

- Think about your own figure shape. Do you have a high or low waistline? Are you an hourglass, apple or straight up and down? How will it sit on your frame?

- Will lengthening the main torso affect the proportions of any other details, such as a ribbed waistline/hem-band?

- What will you be wearing with it?

Keeping a vintage look versus comfort

You are looking to achieve a balance between a garment that you feel comfortable wearing and one that stays as true as possible to the shape and proportions of the original. In the case of jumpers the last question is particularly pertinent – currently trouser waistbands tend to be a lot lower, and you do not want to be constantly tugging at your jumper hemline because you are uncomfortable. On the other hand, if you lengthen the garment too much you are in danger of compromising the vintage look and proportions.

If you are in any doubt, have a recap on 'A guide to twentieth-century knitting fashions' on page 10. For example, we learnt from that section that during the 1950s the inverted triangle was the fashionable shape at the time – will lengthening your 1950s jumper detract from that sculptural impact?

Ribbed welts

Deep, ribbed hemlines were a common feature in the 1940s and 1950s and can really help to define the waistline. For example, the length measurement breakdown from the original pattern might be as follows: 4in (10cm) ribbed hemline + 8in (20cm) main pattern to armhole + 7in (17.5cm) armhole to shoulder.

The ribbed hemline takes up one third of the length from hemline to armhole, so if you are adding an extra 2 to 3in (5 to 7.5cm) in that area, there will obviously be an impact on the narrow waist emphasis – you might want to consider adding some length to the hemline too. Remember, the length of the waistband ribbing could also affect the balance of any sleeve cuff ribbing, so if you do increase the ribbed rows you may want to add some length into the cuff ribs too.

Allowing for patterns & style details

Another consideration is whether or not your garment is knitted in a particular stitch pattern or Fair Isle – how deep is that pattern? Will you be able to accommodate an extra repeat if you are adding to the length?

Lengthening the garment can also alter other style details – for instance, you might have a sports jumper with a small collar and buttoned neck opening that extends 5in (12.5cm) down into the jumper. If you have lengthened the torso but not the neck opening, you are in danger of affecting the balance between the top and bottom and will end up with acres of blank torso topped by a tiny opening that may look off-balance.

SEE ALSO *Taking your measurements, page 30, Deconstruct to reconstruct, page 32, Adjusting armholes & sleeves, page 64, Working with Fair Isles & stitch patterns, page 82*

The original length of this jumper from *Vogue Knitting* No. 35 (1949) was a little short on me so I lengthened the torso, ensuring the yoke/torso proportion was retained.

LENGTHENING ARMHOLES

Do not forget that a certain amount of negative ease should be accounted for here, and the tight-fitting jumper is not meant to compare to our looser jumpers today, so you do not want to lose that fitted look altogether. However, you might decide that you would actually prefer to move your arms freely rather than having them glued to your sides, in which case, adjust away.

Lengthening armholes is not the difficult part, particularly when it is a plain yoke – just calculate how much extra length you need and knit extra rows accordingly. There are, however, some things you need to bear in mind:

- When you adjust the main body armhole measurements, you will need to adjust the sleeve shape to match. This will impact short-sleeved patterns more than long-sleeved ones – you might end up with a sleeve that ends at the elbow rather than the halfway mark between shoulder and elbow.

- Take into account any stitch or colourwork patterns – a patterned or textured yoke was pretty common during the 1930s and 1940s.

- Remember that you will have to incorporate any button or front opening devices into your new length.

Pro tip

If you are lengthening a cardigan or other garment with buttons, you will have to re-space the buttonholes. If you have lengthened it by a significant amount, think about adding in an extra buttonhole.

Adjusting armholes & sleeves

Sleeve design can be the most complicated part of a garment, but the illustrations I will use here will show you some simpler solutions. You will need to make sleeve and armhole adjustments when you have made alterations to the torso/bust and shoulder widths, or when you have adjusted the depth from armhole-shaping to shoulder.

WORKING OUT SLEEVE SHAPES

There are several different theories you can apply to sleeve design (particularly fitted sleeves), which can make it a confusing area and worthy of a book in itself. There is even specific computer software to help you, or you can go to websites where you enter your measurements and the desired sleeve shape is automatically calculated for you (see 'Useful resources', page 160).

The perfectionist will use trigonometric calculations to determine the curve of the armhole shape cut out of the body (or armscye) and corresponding sleeve shape, but you can simplify matters by breaking down the sleeve anatomy and committing what you know to knitter's graph paper, then re-plotting it using your own measurements.

Here we will look at some of the most prevalent sleeve shapes you are likely to find.

Pro tip

I prefer to plot my sleeve shaping from the top so I work out the final width of my sleeve (the cast-off edge), the height of the sleeve crown, the upper arm width (before shaping), the cast-on edge width, and plot the curved shaping (increases/decreases).

Right: These two late 1930s/early 1940s jumper patterns use the classic fitted sleeve for a simple silhouette, adding unusual pockets and slightly more elaborate neckline designs to give the garments a twist.

Far right: A 1940s Fair Isle jumper uses classic fitted sleeves, the most common sleeve style you will come across in vintage patterns.

FITTED SLEEVES

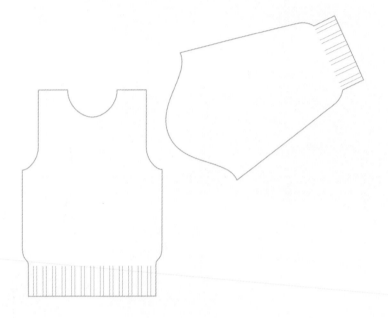

The most common sleeve type in vintage patterns is a fitted sleeve. From the late 1950s onwards, a simpler dropped shoulder or slightly indented square sleeve was common, but the fitted sleeve follows the shape of the body more closely and eliminates excess underarm bulk.

The fitted sleeve shape and its corresponding body armhole can be seen in the illustration above. The perimeter of the sleeve crown, or cap, matches the size of the armhole, sometimes with a little extra at the crown to help ease it in when sewn. The shaping can match the body's armhole, or it can differ slightly.

We are used to more ease around the armhole in our modern clothing, whereas many vintage knits can seem a little too tight in this area for our comfort – the usual result of both smaller-sized bodies and the insistence on emphasising a close fit.

Guidelines for the armhole

You will be guided by your pattern as to how the sleeve is shaped, but here are a few general guidelines for the fitted sleeve armhole:

- The shaping is typically worked over 1½ to 3in (3.8 to 7.4cm) in length.

- The armhole is worked in three stages: initial cast-off, steep decrease and straight ascent without shaping.

- The first stage contains a certain number of cast-off stitches that will measure ½ to 1in (1.3 to 2.5cm) in width at each side.

- The number of stitches cast off over the first two rows of armhole shaping can often be up to half of the entire amount to be decreased (see example below).

Guidelines for the sleeve

Here are some guidelines for the sleeve itself:

- The term 'crown', or 'cap', refers to the length that starts at the armhole shaping and ends at the sleeve cast-off.

- The armhole depth and the sleeve width are often directly related: the sleeve can be approximately twice as wide as the armhole is deep, e.g. a 14in- (35cm-) wide upper sleeve will form a crown that will neatly fit a 7in- (17.5cm-) deep armhole; in vintage patterns the sleeve width can vary slightly.

- The sleeve's shaping is worked in four stages: initial cast-off, steep decrease, shallow decrease and cast-off.

- The crown height should be about three quarters of the armhole depth, e.g. for an 8in- (20cm-) deep armhole, the cap should be about 5½in (13.75cm) tall (although this can vary).

- The width at the top of the crown can be between 2 and 6in (5 and 15cm) depending on sleeve width and bust size.

- Generally the body's armhole shaping can be the same as the initial sleeve's shaping, although it may differ slightly.

Assessing the pattern

In order to assess how we will make our adjustments, you need to look at your original pattern and work out how it was designed, keeping an eye on the shaping proportions.

Let us take the armhole and sleeve shaping from a 1952 *Stitchcraft* pattern as an example. From the pattern we can deduce the following.

- The tension is 8 stitches and 10 rows to the inch (2.5cm).

- Although the pattern gives the bust measurement as 34 to 35in (85 to 87.5cm), it actually works out to 33½in (83.75cm), giving a −½ to 1½in (1.25 to 3.75cm) negative ease.

- The armhole depth is 8in (20cm).

- We want to adapt the main body of the jumper to fit a 36 to 37in (90 to 92.5cm) bust with the same negative ease (a bust width increase of 2in [5cm]) while retaining the shoulder and neck widths, and also to increase the depth of the armhole to 8½in (21.25cm).

The pattern reads as follows:

Shape armholes (stitch count prior to armhole shaping: 134 sts)

Cast off 8 sts at beg of next 2 rows

K2tog at each end of every row until 102 sts remain (16 rows = 1.6in [4cm])

Work straight until back measures 20in (62 rows = 6.2in [15.5cm])

Shape sleeves (stitch count prior to crown/cap shaping: 100 sts)

Shape top by casting off 4 sts at beg of next 2 rows

K2tog at each end of every knit row until 48 sts remain (48 rows = 4.8in [12cm])

K2tog at each end of every row until 24 sts (3in [7.5cm]) remain (12 rows = 1.2in [3cm])

Cast off

Putting it on paper

If you look at the illustration on the facing page, you can see how it looks on knitter's graph paper – by using the tension guide I worked out the corresponding measurements. You will see that the height of the sleeve crown does not initially seem to correspond to the armhole height; this is accounted for by the fact that the cast-off edge at the top of the sleeve will constitute part of the sleeve height when it is sewn into the armhole and the curved shape. The cast-off edge measurement will be distributed equally over the back and front of the shoulder, so you will need to divide that in half and add it to your sleeve-crown height.

The other thing you will notice is that the armhole casts off eight stitches at the beginning of the first two rows, while the sleeve casts off four stitches. You will come across this from time to time: whether or not the initial armhole and sleeve shaping are the same can depend on the width and height of the sleeve (i.e. how many rows the sleeve has to make its decreases).

In this example, we cast off 24 stitches (3in or 7.5cm) for the sleeve, which gives us an extra 1½in (3.75cm) to add to the sleeve-crown height of 6¼in (15.5cm). We can calculate that the armhole height is 8in (20cm), while the sleeve-crown height is 7¾in (19.25cm) by adding 6¼in (15.5cm) to 1½in (3.75cm).

This 1930s jumper combines an unusual bodice design (knitted from left to right instead of the usual bottom to top) with traditional ribbed welt and fitted sleeves.

Another useful proportion to note here is the number of stitches cast off at the beginning of the shaping. For the armhole we need to decrease 32 stitches overall before working straight again: we cast off 16 stitches altogether at the initial cast off over the first two rows, which is exactly half of the stitches to be decreased overall. Referring back to our guidelines you will see that this is a common rule of thumb, so that is something that you will want to replicate in your own armhole shaping.

Re-plotting your measurements

Next we are going to re-plot our body armhole and sleeve using our revised measurements. We will take the measurements we know, which are the number of cast-off stitches over the first two rows of the armhole and the armhole height.

To decide how many stitches we want to cast off at the top of the sleeve, we will establish a rough ratio of sleeve-crown height (excluding cast-off edge) to armhole height – in this case the sleeve-crown height is about three quarters of the armhole height, which means

the cast-off edge measures about one quarter. Since we are only adding ½in (from 8 to 8½in), we will add two extra stitches to the cast-off edge.

Finally we will plot a line from the cast off stitches to the top of the sleeve crown, and the shoulder of the armhole. To a certain extent you will be guided by your pattern and will see a rhythm forming where the decreases are steep or shallow – allow this to guide you using your revised measurements so that the shape you end up with is as similar to the original pattern as possible.

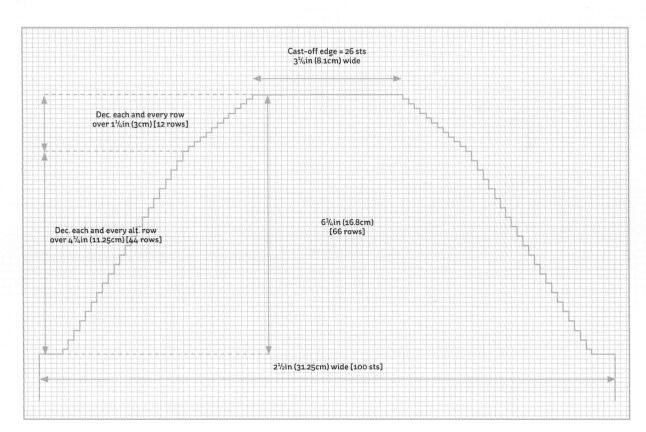

Cast-off edge = 26 sts
3¼in (8.1cm) wide

Dec. each and every row over 1¼in (3cm) [12 rows]

Dec. each and every alt. row over 4¾in (11.25cm) [44 rows]

6¾in (16.8cm) [66 rows]

2½in (31.25cm) wide [100 sts]

The instructions for the sleeve are translated into the actual shape and measurements.

BOX-HEAD SLEEVES/STRAIGHT-EDGED SLEEVES

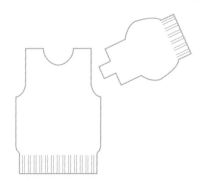

Box-head sleeves were most popular during the 1940s when a square-shaped torso was all-important. As with fitted sleeves, they tend to be worn snugly under the arm, so always check the armhole measurements before you start a pattern to check you are comfortable with the fit.

Our 'Tea-Time Jumper' uses box-head sleeves to great effect – these are actually pretty easy to adapt as the shaping is made over the first few rows of the armhole rather than gradually throughout the length of it, and the rest of the sleeve is knitted without shaping to fit into a straight armhole.

You will see from the illustration left that the sleeve head is made to create the shape of a box. After knitting the initial sleeve crown, roughly one third of the stitches are cast off at either side, leaving the remaining central stitches to create the top of the box. The length of the box top is equal to the width created by the cast-off stitches so that they match when sewn together (see illustration on the facing page).

This is a nice simple sleeve to alter. The sleeve will take its lead from the changes made to the main body's armhole, so we will start with those armhole changes.

Armhole shaping

You may remember when we looked at width adjustments (see page 56) that you ended up with more stitches at the beginning of your armhole shaping to accommodate a wider bust measurement. However, you need to get rid of those surplus stitches to end up with the same shoulder measurements as the original, which we will do at the initial armhole-shaping stage.

The pattern tells us to cast off 6 stitches at the beginning of the following four rows: if we stuck to that we would end up with 12 stitches too many at the shoulder cast-off stage, so we will need to cast off an extra 6 stitches. We could do this in two ways:

- Lose them by casting off 6 stitches at the beginning of the following six instead of four rows.

- Do it more gradually by casting off 6 stitches at the beginning of the next four rows (per the pattern), and then decrease one stitch at each end of the following three rows.

I went for the former option to preserve the slightly tighter underarm appearance.

The second change I made to the armhole was to lengthen it just slightly. I did not want to lose the fitted effect of the blouse entirely and spoil the look, but I did want to feel comfortable, so I added an extra ¾in (1.8cm) to the armhole length – according to my row tension calculations this translated as an extra eight rows of pattern.

So we have ended up with a longer armhole and extra shaping that we will now need to accommodate in the sleeve itself. It gets interesting here – since the sleeve shaping echoes the armhole (per the pattern), I will need to repeat the curve by casting off 6 stitches at the beginning of the next six rows (a total of 36 stitches that we cast off at the start of the armhole), but I want to preserve the rest of the sleeve size and proportions.

The original sleeve pattern tells us to cast on 98 stitches and decrease down to 74 stitches – if I cast off 36 stitches per my revised armhole shaping, I will end up with 62 stitches after shaping, which will mean the sleeve will be too narrow.

The pattern for the bottom of the sleeve tells us to knit for 4in (10cm) without shaping – according to our row tension this gives us 40 rows over which to increase 12 stitches. I divide the 12 in half (as we will be increasing at each end of the row, 2 stitches per row) and calculate as shown in equation A:

So I will increase 1 stitch at each end of every sixth row, meaning I will be up to 110 stitches by row 36, then continue straight until row 40. For the shaping I will then be able to cast off the 6 stitches over the next six rows and still end up with 74 stitches. It is not absolutely ideal as it will give the bottom part of the sleeve a bit of tapering it is not meant to have, but the effect on the overall garment is minimal.

If my upper arm circumference measurement had been greater than that of the pattern, I could have included those extra stitches at cast-on stage, but I wanted to keep the circumference the same. I have also decided to keep the cast-off edge the same as the original – any more and the 'box' would then have become much wider and out of proportion.

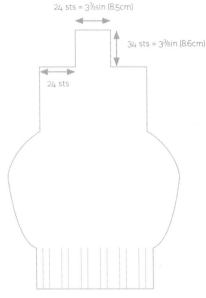

24 sts = 3⁷⁄₁₆in (8.5cm)

34 sts = 3⅜in (8.6cm)

24 sts

Calculations

A.

40 [rows]

÷

6 [stitch increase rows]

=

6.66 [which I round down to 6]

Pro tip

To widen a gathered sleeve, you need to either continue the extra width through to the cast-off edge (which means more fabric to ease in) or include further decreases in your shaping, resulting in the same number of cast-off stitches as the original pattern.

GATHERED (PUFF) OR PLEATED CROWN

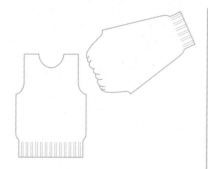

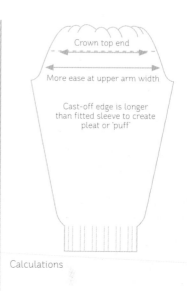

Crown top end

More ease at upper arm width

Cast-off edge is longer than fitted sleeve to create pleat or 'puff'

Calculations

Another familiar vintage feature, this style is very similar to the fitted sleeve but with a wider cast-off edge resulting in additional fabric that is then gathered or pleated to ease into the armhole (see illustration left). This extra bit of forgiving ease makes the adaptation slightly easier as you have scope to adjust the fit.

Puff and pleated cap sleeves can be designed with traditional shaped edges (as for the fitted sleeve), or with a straighter crown with no shaping (as for the box-head sleeve), so when it comes to adaptation you can follow the instructions given for the fitted and box-head sleeves, bearing in mind that the cast-off edge needs up to 30 per cent more than the average fitted sleeve.

CAP SLEEVES

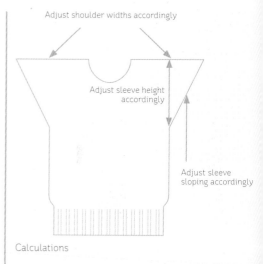

Adjust shoulder widths accordingly

Adjust sleeve height accordingly

Adjust sleeve sloping accordingly

Calculations

The cap sleeve enjoyed its heyday in the 1950s, emphasising a small waist and a slender arm. You will find they are often knitted integrally as part of the body, although they can be fitted separately, making their adaptation very straightforward (see illustration right). The sleeve can end just below the armhole shaping, or just above it. It is worked by widening the garment through increases instead of decreases at the usual armhole-shaping stage.

The sleeve is most likely to include some shaping in the form of step decreases at the shoulder so that it moulds itself closer to the body. Adjustments to cap sleeves that are designed as an extension to the body are pretty straightforward: to lengthen their depth you will need to start the increases sooner than the original and incorporate the increases into your revised crown measurement.

To adjust the shoulder width, you will need to ascertain where the shaping decreases occur by plotting them out on knitter's graph paper, then re-plotting them using your own measurements.

This 1940s jumper uses an inverted 'V' ribbed waistband to give it shape. This is often a good place to add length (see the original pattern image on page 100).

LEG OF MUTTON

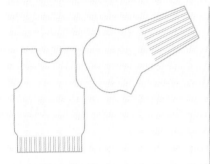

Similar to the gathered sleeve top, but this sleeve is taken to an exaggerated extreme and made even more voluminous by a tight-fitting (usually ribbed) bottom section. The fitted section runs from the elbow to wrist, sometimes a few inches above the elbow to make a larger puffed section at the top (see illustration left).

Adjustments can be made to them according to whether they are set-in or straight-edged (generally the latter). Make sure you have swatched up the bottom part of the sleeve to ensure a good tight fit that will go over your hand and elbow comfortably and also allow ease of movement.

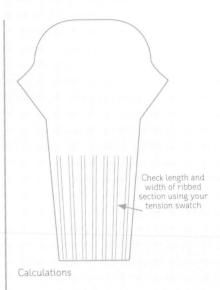

Check length and width of ribbed section using your tension swatch

Calculations

DOLMAN SLEEVES

Dolman or batwing sleeves became more common in knitting patterns during the 1950s. The armhole measurement is a lot deeper than the average fitted sleeve, and the sleeve slots into the body at a steep angle (see illustration right). They are often worked integrally as part of the main body.

Their extra depth and width generally mean that adjustments to armhole depth will not be necessary. If you do find you need to adapt them, it will usually be a case of adding extra width to the garment's main body, then making corresponding underarm adjustments accordingly (as for the straight-edged sleeve). Another thing to check is that the wrist circumference measurement matches your own.

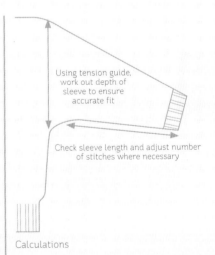

Using tension guide, work out depth of sleeve to ensure accurate fit

Check sleeve length and adjust number of stitches where necessary

Calculations

RAGLAN SLEEVES

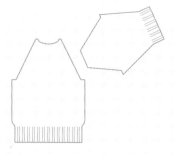

Like the dolman, raglan sleeves were rarely seen in knitting patterns prior to the 1950s (although they were featured in leisure and sportswear). The sleeves are joined to the body at an angle, creating a diagonal seam from the underarm to the shoulder (see illustration above). Here are some guidelines.

- The number of rows in the sleeve crown and armhole must be identical.

- A raglan armhole can measure 1 to 3in (2.5 to 7.5cm) deeper than the classic fitted sleeve to allow for movement.

- The upper arm width can measure about 1in (2.5cm) more than the classic fitted sleeve.

- The top of the raglan sleeve (cast-off edge) can measure from 1 to 3in (2.5 to 7.5cm).

In most cases you should not need to adapt a raglan sleeve crown and width as the extra depth and ease can be accommodated in a more modern figure (bearing in mind that this style became fashionable at a time when patterns were just beginning to cater for measurements larger than the traditional 34in [85cm] bust).

The best approach to adapting raglan sleeves is to plot out the original instructions on knitter's graph paper to work out its anatomy, and re-adjust accordingly.

If you would like to find out more about adapting raglan sleeves, see 'Useful resources' on page 160.

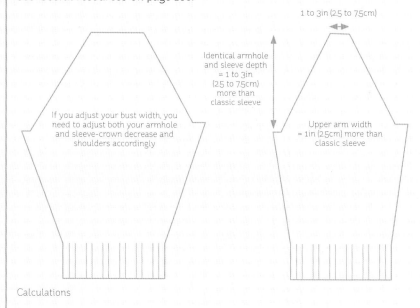

1 to 3in (2.5 to 7.5cm)

Identical armhole and sleeve depth = 1 to 3in (2.5 to 7.5cm) more than classic sleeve

If you adjust your bust width, you need to adjust both your armhole and sleeve-crown decrease and shoulders accordingly

Upper arm width = 1in (2.5cm) more than classic sleeve

Calculations

Adjusting shoulders

You will be guided by your pattern as to the shoulder shape, but the main measurements are the ones you have to watch: you will often need to adjust your shoulder widths, either because the measurements do not match your own or due to neckline adjustments. Here we will have a look at some general rules that apply to the most common shoulder shapes: sloped and straight.

STRAIGHT SHOULDERS

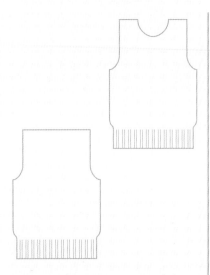

This gives the garment a square shape (see illustrations above) and was particularly popular in the 1940s with the square, boxy look (see the 'Tea-Time Jumper'). Straight shoulders were often used with collared jumpers as the higher back neck prevents the collar from sagging. Calculate the width of the shoulders using your tension as a guide and compare it with your own shoulder dimensions using your measurements table.

There is a direct relation between the bust measurement you end up with before armhole shaping and your shoulder measurements. The number of stitches you have on your needle at the widest part of your bust measurement will need to be decreased accordingly at the armhole-shaping stage to end up with the correct shoulder widths.

I was happy with the measurements for the 'Tea-Time Jumper' and the neckline was to remain the same width, so it was a case of making sure I ended up with the same number of stitches on the needle at cast-off stage. As we saw from the 'Adjusting armholes & sleeves' section, I started off with more stitches than the original at the bust so I had to decrease at the armhole-shaping stage by 12 stitches, to avoid ending up with shoulders that were at least 1in (2.5cm) wider than my own.

If my shoulder measurements had been wider or narrower, I would have incorporated them appropriately into my armhole shaping.

SLOPING SHOULDERS

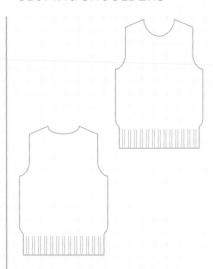

Imagine the slope of your shoulder as a triangle inside a rectangle (see illustration on facing page).

- Measurement A is the base of the triangle (from where the neck joins the shoulder parallel to the point fractionally past where your arm begins).

- Measurement B is the height from where the neck joins the shoulder, to the point equal to your shoulder height.

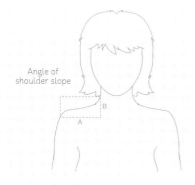

Angle of shoulder slope

My own shoulder rectangle measurement, for instance, is as follows:

A = 5in (12.5cm)
B = 2in (5cm)

From your measurements table you know that your back width is, say, 16in (40cm) and your neck hole requirement is 6in (15cm), which equal 112 stitches and 42 stitches respectively (according to our tension guideline of 7 stitches to the inch (2. 5cm).

You then perform the calculations shown in equation A. We need to round that down to an even number, which gives us 34 stitches available to create the slope for each shoulder.

Next we need to calculate how many rows are available to us to create the slope. This is simply a case of taking measurement B from the illustration above, rounding it down by ½in (1cm) to account for the flexibility of the knitted fabric and multiplying it by our row tension. In this instance it will appear as given in equation B.

Since we can only cast off at the beginning of alternate rows, we are going to divide that by 2, meaning we have ten rows over which to make the slope.

Finally, we need to decide how to divide up our cast-off stitches to give us our slope. Following the calculation given in equation C:

Since this leaves us with a remainder we will round it down to 3. Do not forget we are working the cast-offs over every alternate row so we will need to cast off double that amount on each shaping row. However, if we were to cast off 3 stitches at the beginning of the next ten alternate rows, we would only end up casting off 30 stitches instead of 34, so we will break the steps down as follows.

Row 1: Cast off 6 sts at shoulder edge

Next and every foll alt row: Knit

Row 3: Cast off 6 sts at shoulder edge

Row 5: Cast off 6 sts at shoulder edge

Row 7: Cast off 8 sts at shoulder edge

Row 9: Cast off rem 10 sts

A.

112 [number of back stitches]
−
42 [number of neck hole stitches]
=
70 sts [total number of shoulder stitches]
÷
2
=
35 [stitches per shoulder]

B.

2in (5cm) [shoulder depth]
×
10 [row tension]
=
20 [rows available for shaping]

C.

34 [number of stitches available]
÷
10 [number of rows available]
=
3.4

Adjusting necklines

There are times when you find that the neckline in the original pattern is a little too narrow or shallow for your liking. When planning your neckline alterations, it is good to have an understanding of how they are created in the first place, so that you can start from scratch with your own adaptations.

GETTING STARTED

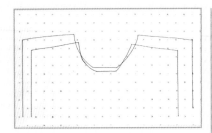

There are many different necklines, but shown here are the three basic shapes that form the basis for other necklines: crew neck, square neck and V-neck.

As before, a very simple way to work out the neckline is by using knitter's graph or dressmaker's spot-and-cross paper. You can plot new points around the original measurements and join the dots accordingly, creating the shapes as you go that you will then translate into instructions. Alternatively, follow the steps below.

HOW TO CREATE A CREW NECK

The classic crew neck is a hole scooped out of the front of a jumper and fitted fairly close to the neck (see illustration above). To calculate the depth of the crew neck you need first to measure from the point at which your neck meets your shoulder to the point parallel to where your shoulder ends (measurement B in the illustration on page 77).

When you calculate your neck depth, remember to accommodate any ribbing or finishing stitch you might be using at the edge.

Next you need to establish a neck width measurement that you are comfortable with. I rarely encourage people to use modern garment measurements when planning out vintage knitwear, but in this case a close-fitting T-shirt will give you a measurement that you know you are comfortable with. The jersey material has a similar elasticity to the knitted fabric so will be a close approximation.

In this example we are going to assume the following:

- Our neck width is 6in (15cm)
- Our shoulder width is 5in (12.5cm)
- The neck depth is 2in (5cm)
- The neck rib is 1in (2.5cm) deep
- The total neckline depth is therefore 3in (7.5cm)
- Our tension is 8 stitches and 10 rows to the inch
- The garment is 128 stitches wide at the point where the neck commences

To shape the neckline, you need to calculate how many rows deep and how many stitches wide it will be by using your tension as shown in equations A and B.

You have 30 rows available to decrease 48 stitches. If you use the classic 'dec 1 st each side of every other row', this means you have 15 rows available.

To work out how many stitches to place on a holder for the centre neck, follow the calculation in equation C. The number of stitches you cast off initially should equal roughly one third of the total number you need to cast off.

To calculate how far into your row you need to begin your neck shaping, perform the calculations given in equations D, E and F.

So your instructions will be as follows.

K55 sts, place the following 18 sts on stitch holder, K55 sts

Cont on one shoulder, dec 1 st on alternate rows until 40 sts remain for shoulder (neck measures 2in [5cm] from beginning of shaping)

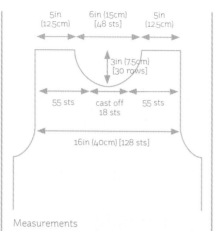

Measurements

A.

Width
8 [sts per inch]
×
6 [neck width
in inches]
=
48 sts

B.

Height
3 [neck depth]
×
10 [rows per inch]
=
30 rows deep

C.

48 [neck hole sts]
−
30 rows [neck depth]
=
18 [stitches on holder]

D.

128 [garment width in sts]
÷
2
=
64 [this is your centre line]

E.

18 [stitches on holder]
÷
2
=
9

F.

64 [centre line]
−
9 [half the stitches on the holder]
=
55

HOW TO CREATE A SQUARE NECK

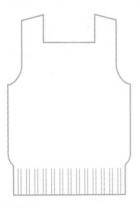

To work out how many stitches to knit either side, calculate as given in equation A.

So your instructions will look as follows:

K40 sts, place the following 48 sts on stitch holder, k40 sts

Cont on each shoulder separately

Sweetheart necklines are also based on a square neck, but they start out wider at the base of the shaping and get narrower as they reach the shoulder. These are easily integrated into your calculations. They can also include a dip at the centre of the neckline to give a heart shape.

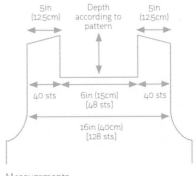

Measurements

Square-neck adaptations are very similar to crew-neck adaptations, although they tend to be deeper than the average crew neck (see illustration above). You can work out from your pattern how deep the neck should be (although if you have altered the length of the garment you should make sure you keep the neck depth proportional to the new overall length).

Calculate the neck width as for the crew-neck adjustments (remembering to include any rib), but this time the amount of stitches you place on the stitch holder will be the total neck width (in our crew neck example, this will be 48 stitches).

A.

48 [number of neck hole sts]

÷

2

=

24

64 [centre line]

−

24 [half the neck hole stitches]

=

40

Pro tip

Rather than making your shaping at the very edge of your neckline (i.e. last or first stitch), try making your increases or decreases one or two stitches before you get to the edge: this gives a firmer, cleaner edge.

HOW TO CREATE A V-NECK

This is actually fairly straightforward to work out but you will need a central point in your garment upon which to base your 'V', which means an odd number of stitches. If you have not planned ahead and have already reached this point with an even number of stitches, you can increase (M1) one stitch where you want your 'V' to begin.

Next you will need to work out the 'V' – as with the square neck, make sure the depth is proportional to any other length adjustments you have made to the overall garment. The length will be measured from the point where the neck meets the shoulder to the base of the 'V'.

We will base our measurements on the previous crew neck example, and will create a 'V' that is 7in (17.5cm) deep. To recap, the neck hole needs to be 6in (15cm) or 48 stitches wide, so we will calculate the number of rows available to us to make our 'V' increases using our stitch tension: 10 × 7 = 70 rows.

You will be working on the V-neck in two halves, one at a time, so divide your design in two and work out the dimensions accordingly. With that in mind, you have 24 stitches to decrease for each half at the neck edge over 70 rows.

To calculate which rows you will be making the decreases on, follow equation A.

Things do not always work out neatly – obviously you cannot work with uneven numbers so you will have to spread your decreases carefully. Assuming that the first decrease will be made on the first row of any shaping, there are a number of choices available:

- You can decrease 2 stitches at the neck edge on every fifth row, leaving 4 rows without shaping at the end.

- You can increase 1 stitch at the neck edge on every alternate row for 21 rows (by which point you will have decreased 11 stitches), then every third row until 60 rows have been completed (24 stitches will have been decreased), leaving 10 rows without shaping at the end.

- You can increase 1 stitch at the neck edge on every third row for 60 rows (21 stitches), then every alternate row until 66 rows have been completed.

These three different methods create very slightly different shaped 'V's – choose the one that suits your pattern best.

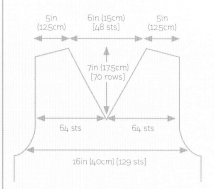

Measurements

A.

70 [rows]
÷
24 [sts]
=
2.91

Pro tip

Do not forget, if you alter the width of your neckline, it will have repercussions for your shoulders and any finishing or collar styling (which will need lengthening accordingly), so look ahead and plan the project thoroughly.

Working with Fair Isles & stitch patterns

Let us assume that you have made your width and length adjustments – all were straightforward in stocking/stockinette stitch, but how do you go about accommodating the extra stitches and rows without interrupting the flow of colourwork or stitch patterns? What if your jumper is worked in a geometric contrast design?

FAIR ISLES & COLOURWORK

Fair Isle jumpers and twinsets (often plain with a Fair Isle yoke) were popular during the 1940s when spare or unravelled lengths of coloured wool could be incorporated into a plain garment to give it colour and interest.

Many patterns did not contain a graphic chart for their colourwork, preferring to give the instructions row by row. I recommend that you create your own chart from the original when you come across one of these patterns: not only does it prevent confusion, but it helps when it comes to incorporating extra stitches from any width or length adjustments.

Imagine each Fair Isle stitch group as its own self-contained design that, when repeated, creates a larger composition. The original pattern will generally ensure that the sides of the garment 'frame' the stitch group compositions and that the stitch patterns are centred neatly. When you add a few extra stitches to make the garment wider, your pattern will be thrown out so you will need to look at the best way to re-centre the design.

STITCH PATTERNS

For this section we are going to use our 'Tea-Time Jumper' pattern, which uses a 'pyramid' stitch throughout, as an example. Stitch patterns are much the same as Fair Isles in that they are worked in formal groups that are then repeated regularly, so we are dealing with a similar procedure.

First of all you have to work out how many stitches are in the pattern group. You may be able to do this by reading through the instructions thoroughly and working it out at a glance, particularly when the stitch is a simple one, but in this instance I preferred to work it out on paper.

I calculated that the pattern covered a 12-stitch group, plus 2 extra stitches at the beginning of the row to balance it up (like Fair Isle, stitch patterns are 'framed' centrally).

My width adjustments resulted in 14 extra stitches to add to the garment: this meant that I could comfortably accommodate an extra stitch pattern group with 2 stitches to spare. To continue the central framing device I divided those 2 stitches up and added one extra to the beginning and end of the rows.

This classic late 1940s/early 1950s pattern uses a bright band of Fair Isle colourwork at the neck, above the sleeve welts and above the deep, ribbed waist.

What to do when revisions are not straightforward

This works fine when your revisions are neatly and comfortably incorporated, but that will not always be the case. What if my width adjustments had resulted in 8 extra stitches? There would have been two options available to me:

- I could keep the original number of pattern repeats and 'frame' them by adding 4 extra plain stitches to each side of the design.

- I could incorporate the extra stitches by adding half a stitch pattern to either side of the garment.

This is a decision I faced when it came to the front of the garment – you will see that the jumper has a central panel with fake buttons, either side of which is half a stitch group. I wanted to keep that motif but it did not fit neatly into my revised design with extra stitches, so I had to create half a stitch pattern at either side of the pattern.

These will be the decisions facing you with your own stitch pattern alterations: a case of keeping the balance between a central and evenly spaced design and your revised stitch count. As ever, the more projects you work on the easier it becomes and you will become adept at working out the best, most visually appealing solution.

The stitch pattern on our 'Tea-Time Jumper' was revised to accommodate the width adjustments.

Pro tip

If you are in doubt about the overall effect of your colourwork or stitch pattern adjustments, consider investing a bit of extra time in your project by knitting up the relevant section of the garment to see if the adjustments will work.

CONTRAST COLOUR SHAPES

This great 1950s jumper offers a twist on the two-colour yoke by creating three triangular peaks of the main colour, lending the garment a bodice effect. It is for a 34in (86cm) bust, which is too small for my 36in (91cm) frame, so I am going to have to re-work those points. The tension is 9 stitches to the inch.

The colour is worked using separate balls of yarn and occurs at the beginning of the armhole shaping. We have 153 stitches on the needle, and the colourwork instructions read as follows:

K19W, k32B, k1W, k32B, k1W, k32B, k19

The points are knitted over 16 rows.

By increasing the bust width by 2in (5cm), I will be adding an extra 18 stitches, which results in 9 stitches to each side of the garment. I will round this down to 8 to keep it even and divisible by 2 (the stitches will be either side of the garment). Since it is only a few stitches I will add 4 stitches to the straight line either side of the triangular peaks, so the instructions will read as follows:

K23W, k32B, k1W, k32B, k1W, k32B, k23W

For a larger bust

For example, what if I was designing for a 40in (100cm) bust? This would mean an extra 54 stitches (or 27 stitches to each side). If I round that down to 26 stitches, this would mean adding an extra 13 stitches to each side of the shaping, which may

A 1950s pattern using geometric peaks in contrasting colours to separate the yoke from the body.

start to look a little odd. Another option is possible here: we could incorporate some of the extra stitches in the triangular points over a few more rows.

I know there are three points to the triangles, each with a base line of 32 stitches. I need to accommodate 26 stitches over the three triangles – 26 is not divisible by 3 (it leaves a total of 8 with 2 remaining), so I will incorporate the extra 2 stitches into either side of the point shaping. Our instructions will now look as follows:

K24W, k40B, k1W, k40B, k1W, k40B, k24W

Now you may have noticed something... this will make our points a bit taller (8 rows, or just over 1in [2.5cm]). In this case, if you have not already added some length to your jumper, you may want to think about it to balance out your adjustments and make sure they are visually in proportion – for instance, you could add some extra length to the armhole and main torso in equal amounts.

Case study: working with Fair Isle

Let us take a classic WWII-era jumper with a Fair Isle yoke as our example (see photo above).

The pattern is uncharted but we will get an idea of how the design should look from the pattern picture. It is also common for patterns from this era to suggest which colours you should use; this one suggests natural (N), black (B), blue (Bl) and red (R), which I have decided to stick to.

The Fair Isle pattern runs for 20 rows as follows:

Row 1: K thus, 2N, *3B, 2N; rep from * to end of row

Row 2: P thus, 2B, *3Bl, 2B; rep from * to end of row

Row 3: K in Bl

Row 4: P thus, 1R, (1Bl, 1R) 3 times, *3Bl, 1R, (1Bl, 1R) 3 times; rep from * to end of row

Row 5: K thus, (1Bl, 2R) twice, *2Bl, 1R, 2Bl, 2R, 1Bl, 2R; rep from *, ending with 1Bl

Row 6: P thus, 3R, 1N, 3R, *1N, 1R, (1N, 3R) twice; rep from * to end of row

Row 7: K thus, 3N, 1B, 3N, *3B, 3N, 1B, 3N; rep from * to end of row

Now rep. the 6th, 5th, 4th, 3rd, 2nd and 1st rows in this order

Row 14: P in N

Row 15: K thus, 1R, 5N, *2R, 1N, 2R, 5N; rep from *, ending with 1R

Row 16: P thus, 1R, 1Bl, 3R, 1Bl, *2R, 1Bl, 2R, 1Bl, 3R, 2Bl, rep from *, ending with 1R

Row 17: K thus, 3 Bl, 1B, *4Bl, 1B; rep from *, ending with 3 Bl

Now rep the 16th & 15th rows in this order

Row 20: P in N

Case study continued

I worked out that the pattern spans a 10-stitch cluster, whipped out the graph paper and marked out 20 rows for a single pattern set, plus a central panel of 20 squares (by charting more than one pattern group you get a better idea of what the overall design will look like), with a few either side for the entrances and exits to the rows. Time to get out the coloured pencils and colour in each 'stitch' square per the instructions (see chart). I have not used any technical knitting chart symbols here – this is a straightforward colour chart.

I had adapted the pattern to size up the bust, which translated to 6 extra stitches, so I needed to work out how many stitches I would be left with either side of the main group and account for the colourwork accordingly. I halved the 6 to conclude that I would have 3 extra stitches to add to either side of my Fair Isle design, and added three extra squares to my graph paper design. Now it was just a case of working out what the stitch design either side of those main groups would be by looking at the main group pattern.

You might find that in some instances that you end up with enough extra stitches to include an extra pattern repeat.

Finally, a word about including extra rows. In this instance I did not need to add any extra length to the armhole, but had I needed to I would have had two options:

- Continue per the pattern, but incorporate extra patterned rows at the shoulders.

- Incorporate the extra rows in the plain colour section, which would have the effect of pushing the Fair Isle design upwards slightly.

With the second option, make sure that it does not throw out the patterned proportions of the garment too much – if you are not adding much length it should not have too dramatic an effect on the overall design.

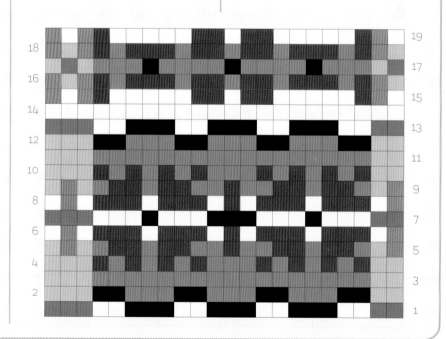

A classic WWII-era jumper with a Fair Isle yoke.

Retro-styling modern patterns

LE BOUTON
de LUXE

SIRDAR

4. ADJUSTING SIZES

Finding & assessing your pattern

The first step to giving your modern pattern a vintage makeover is to find a suitable 'canvas' on which to project your vintage fantasies. What are we defining as 'modern'? In knitting pattern terms I think of modern as anything from the mid-1970s onwards, as these patterns will cater for more contemporary figures and yarn requirements.

WHY USE A MODERN PATTERN?

Adapting a vintage pattern can be a challenge and many of us do not have the time. If you like the idea of altering aspects of a pattern to suit your taste without the bother of delving too deep into re-sizing and updating yarn, this option is for you.

The idea behind a vintage makeover of a modern pattern is not to create a perfect replica of a retro garment, but to take details and elements from the plethora of wonderful twentieth-century designs available and blend them into a modern garment using modern yarn that will sit happily in your twenty-first-century wardrobe and on your twenty-first-century body.

The idea of 'pimping' a modern pattern might also appeal to your recycling ethic: there are many patterns that are unloved, unvalued and overlooked and there are mountains of them out there. Why not seize your innate creativity and breathe new life back into them, lovingly moulding them to suit your own vintage aesthetic?

In this section of the book we will be looking at a retro-styled jumper knitted from a modern pattern from start to finish as an example of where your imagination can take you.

This 1980s pattern for a Fair Isle jumper could have come straight from the 1940s. Handily for us, it uses modern measurements, modern ease and modern yarns.

Pro tip

Do not feel you need to throw every vintage detail you can think of at your garment – sometimes just a puff sleeve combined with a contrast yoke is all you need to lend your garment a slice of the elegant simplicity typical of many mid-twentieth-century designs.

Patons

4 PLY

Puff sleeves give your garment an instant retro look.

This pretty sweetheart neckline is a great example of vintage detailing.

Vertical darts accentuate the waistline, hinting at a fitted vintage silhouette while keeping a modern ease.

Knitting patterns from the 1980s in particular often include features inspired by vintage details, making them a good choice for adapting to retro styles.

SOURCING

Sourcing an appropriate pattern
should prove easier than for a vintage
one. You have probably already got
many modern patterns in your own
collection that might be suitable:
have a look through and you will be
surprised how differently you view
them when you consider making
a few tweaks here and there – even
the most ordinary of patterns can
become an interesting possibility.

Relatives, friends and neighbours
may have prospective candidates
lurking in their attic or garage,
and if that proves fruitless, then
your local charity shop might hold
some treasures.

Local yarn shops will also be a
good source, even ones you have
discounted before due to their lack
of inspiration and choice. Revisit
and have another look at what is
available with your new vintage
goggles on.

The web is, as ever, a good place to
look. There is a whole world of basic
patterns out there on auction sites
that you will not have to enter into
a bidding war over, plus there are
many great free resources on
knitting sites that you would not
normally give a second glance.

Patons

C 4154
28-46 in

DOUBLE KNITTING

This 1980s/1990s cropped-top design might not look vintage at first glance, but look
past the pastel colours and the modern design and you will notice that the zigzag stitch
pattern echoes some classic 1940s patterns.

Vintage yarns can still be sourced if you
are an avid collector; they are particularly
useful if you are trying to track down an
authentic colour palette from source.

ASSESSING YOUR PATTERN

The secret to choosing a suitable modern pattern is the ability to use your imagination and see beyond initial impressions. It is like viewing a house for the first time and seeing beyond the wallpaper and carpets to catch a glimpse of its full potential.

There are a couple of ways to approach these initial stages of pattern assessment:

Have an idea in mind (or better still, a sketch) of the end effect you want to achieve. This might be inspired by a vintage image, or even an original pattern that seems too daunting to adapt from scratch.

Alternatively, take a design lead and feel inspired by the possibilities of a modern pattern's elements.

Starting from a vintage look

Have a look through as many vintage knitting patterns and magazines as you can find, or browse the web to get your creative juices flowing. This illustration shows a page from my knitting notebook in which I sketched out various possibilities when I was planning the jumper for this section of the book.

Starting from a modern look

This can happen more often than you think: sometimes a stitch pattern, sleeve shape or neckline can put you in mind of a bit of 1940s or 1950s styling which is all you need to use as a springboard to launch your re-styled version.

I do not say this often, but the 1980s are a particularly good era for this kind of inspiration. Cast aside the vivid colours, bulky or fluffy yarn preferences, and bold graphic motifs and you will find interesting 1950s-inspired detailing that would look great if you opted for different yarns and added a bit of shaping or cut down the ease slightly (see patterns on pages 90 and 91).

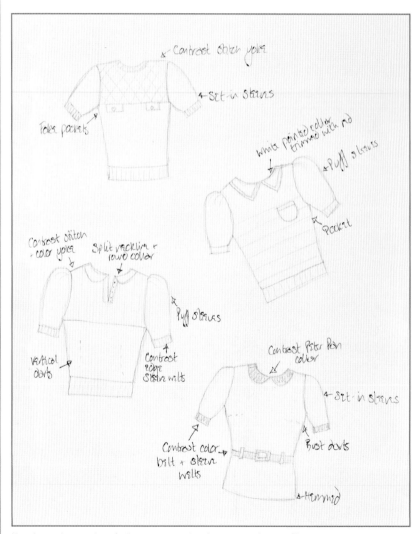

SEE ALSO A brief guide to twentieth-century fashions, page 10, Volume & ease, page 98, Shaping your garment, page 100

You do not have to be a fashion artist to sketch out your designs. These were my initial sketches of some ideas I had for adjusting a modern pattern to include some vintage elements.

Assessing the shape

The first thing I look at is the shape of the garment: I usually opt for something that is simple and classic (and therefore infinitely adaptable). For this section of the book I chose a fairly straightforward pattern for a twinset from the 1990s. It is a pretty design for a cardigan and short-sleeved jumper with fitted sleeves and a lacy pattern at the waist.

The stitch pattern is nice but does not remind me of a vintage garment. The classic, short-sleeved jumper shape, though, strikes me as a perfect background on to which I can pin some classic styling.

There are a few details that I will consider changing at this stage: the shallow ribbed welts might be better with the deeper ribbed waistline so popular in the 1940s and 1950s (plus give extra shaping to the waist). More importantly, its sleeve design (a straightforward fitted sleeve) can form the basis for slightly more elaborate sleeve forms.

This last point is an important one: since we are trying to keep this a simple exercise, you can make the modern pattern work for you by choosing one with a sleeve design you like. The fitted sleeve was the most predominant during the period from the 1930s to the early 1950s and gives you greater flexibility, but the raglan and dolman sleeves did creep in from the mid-1950s onwards. If you are after the latter, find a pattern that already uses that style for your foundation.

Assessing the yarn

Vintage patterns were written with fine yarns in mind, but remember we are not trying to create a perfect replica here. The yarn listed in the pattern is a straightforward DK and the tension guidelines (5.5 stitches/7 rows to the inch on 4mm/US 6 needles) are what you would expect, which will give you lots of possibilities.

The next section will take you through your adjustment considerations and help you to establish a more accurate picture of the original pattern, and decide what kind of changes you might want to make.

DK is a common yarn and is available in a variety of mixtures and colours. It is not an authentic vintage weight, but you can lend your garment a vintage look using other methods.

Adjustment considerations

The idea of adjusting a modern pattern is to make life easier so you do not have to immerse yourself in a complete pattern re-design, but there will be some basic elements that you will want to consider altering to achieve your vintage aim – have fun experimenting!

WHAT DEFINES A VINTAGE GARMENT?

Let us begin by exploring the details that typify a vintage garment:

- Size and shape: we know that vintage patterns tended to cater for smaller bodies, and give a tight-fitting result. This was assisted by the use of negative ease. Garments were generally much shorter than we are used to. Fitted sleeves were also very popular, with varying crown shapes.

- Creative detailing: not that our modern patterns lack this, but there is a certain combination of stitch/sleeve shape/colourwork/ finishing that instantly signals a vintage knit.

- Yarn: vintage patterns up until the beginning of the 1950s used natural fibres (e.g. wool, silk or cotton) with rayon only making an appearance in the 1920s–1930s. They also tended to use a fine yarn, with 2- or 3-ply being the most popular thicknesses.

- Tension: the use of fine yarns meant the use of thin needles and resulted in a fine tension: typically anything from 7 to 9 stitches and 10 rows to the inch were common.

How far should we try and incorporate these details? Well, that is up to you of course, and will depend on the pattern you have chosen to adapt (plus how confident you are feeling), but here are some thoughts to throw into the pot.

Size & shape

We are fortunate that we have such a great range of sizes to choose from. We want to feel comfortable in our garments and one of the advantages of knitting from a modern pattern is that we do not have to worry about negative ease and whether or not we need to wear firm underwear underneath (or if we will be able to squeeze into the garment if we put on a couple of pounds).

Knitting patterns nowadays use an ease allowance (that is to say, the breathing space between your garment and your body) of approximately 2in (5cm), versus vintage patterns which will stray into negative ease (sometimes up to –2in [–2.5cm]). We will look at this in more detail on pages 98 and 99, but you might prefer to preserve the modern ease and find different ways of shaping your garment to simulate a closer fit. Not every pattern design works when it is

sized up, but you can look to the modern patterns to handle this aspect for you.

Garment lengths are also far more accommodating now as our torsos have expanded and trouser/skirt waistlines have become lower. This point is particularly pertinent: our natural waist tends to be somewhere just above the navel and this was the area that was usually dramatically emphasised in knitwear from the 1930s to 1950s. So if we knitted to vintage dimensions, we would end up with a gap between top and bottom.

Although modern patterns tend to include far more detail in their measurement guidelines than older patterns, I recommend you follow the steps in the 'Taking your measurements' section (see page 30) and fill in your own measurements. This useful exercise will give you an idea of which size adjustments you will want to make to your pattern, particularly to the length: you might want to knit 1in (2.5cm) less in the build-up to the armholes as a gesture to vintage proportions, while ensuring that modern comfort is maintained.

Creative detailing

This is one of the things I love most about vintage patterns and is definitely something we can include in our revisions without altering our contemporary version too much. It could be something simple like an unusual cuff, contrast colours or a shoulder fastening with small pearl buttons: it is that extra flourish that means care has been taken and precious time spent – look out for it because it can radically improve the quality of your knitwear.

Again, have a look through as many old patterns as you can to get an idea of what you are aiming for. You can also read through 'A guide to twentieth-century knitting fashions' on page 10 to give you a steer – you will find some highlights from each era that you might want to include in your adaptation (this is also useful for a shape guide). A knitting stitch dictionary and/or Fair Isle book might also come in handy!

We will go into ideas and patterns for some of those details later on to give you a kick-start.

Yarn & tension (gauge)

To a certain extent this will depend on your modern pattern choice. Thicker yarns such as DK are more common today, but you might find some rather nice 4-ply patterns that will get close to the finely knitted fabric found in vintage knits. Be aware that the thicker the yarn the bulkier your fabric, which could affect details such as darts, pleats and sleeve tops.

You could even decide to use a finer yarn and adjust your tension swatch and pattern instructions accordingly, although I think that since this section of the book is about keeping life simple, it would be easier to stick to the yarn weight suggested in the pattern.

Although you are going for a vintage slant, you might want to play around with your colour choices to create a vintage-styled garment with a modern twist. Or maybe the colour choice will be one of the things that give your garment that vintage look, in which case have a look at the 'Colours' section (see page 50).

For our sample pattern I have decided to stick to the DK suggestion to show you how vintage styling can work with modern patterns and yarns. This is one of the main things that will differentiate our modern finished product from a vintage number: the fabric will not be as fine. Be aware that if you do stick to a thicker yarn, there are certain stitches (some of the finer lace ones for example) that will not be as effective, and since it produces a bulkier fabric you will need to keep an eye on details such as puff sleeve caps.

Volume & ease

The definition of 'ease' in fashion design is the amount of space allowed between our body and the garment. Unlike our modern clothes, which generally use a 2 to 4in (5 to 10cm) ease allowance, vintage garments usually ventured into the negative ease territory, which made for tight-fitting knitwear.

CALCULATING EASE

In the previous section we looked at how a distinguishing feature of vintage knitwear was its size and fit. Let us look at that in more detail to find out whether we need to go into adjusting a modern pattern's ease, or if there is a way of avoiding the issue.

The first thing to do is find what the ease allowance is for a modern pattern. When you look at the size guide for your measurements, you will usually see a set of 'Actual measurement' guidelines under the details. The modern pattern we are using as a model has a range of bust sizes from 32/34 to 52/54in (81/86 to 132/137cm). I will be looking at the 36/38in (91/97cm) measurement to suit my own requirements; on closer inspection of the pattern, I find that the actual measurement is 38in (97cm). This means an ease allowance of 2in (5cm) for my measurements.

I am going to double-check that by making my own calculations based on the tension guideline, which is 5.5 stitches and 7 rows to the inch (see equation A).

Multiply the 19½in (48.75cm) for each side by 2, and you reach 39in (97.5cm). This is slightly more than the 'Actual measurements' section tells us, but it does make sense as it gives nearly an inch of ease for the 38in bust measurement. However, this does mean you have an extra 3in (7.5cm) on top of your 36in (91cm) bust.

A.

Number of sts at widest point
÷
sts per inch
=
actual measurement (per side)

In this case it works out at:
107 [number of sts
at widest point]
÷
5.5 [sts per inch]
=
19½ [inches per side]

WHAT TO DO IF THERE IS A DISCREPANCY

If the measurements do not work out, you have a couple of options available to you:

- Accept that your garment will have more ease than a vintage one and find other ways to reflect a vintage shape.

- Explore whether or not you can lessen the ease by looking at the next size down and working out if that is closer to your actual measurements.

Pro tip

Long sleeves need a good fit at the wrist so you will need less ease. Plan on 1in (2.5cm).

SEE ALSO *Taking your measurements,* page 30, *Adjustment considerations,* page 96, *Shaping your garment,* page 100

The second option here is not always possible: for example, the next size down in our pattern is 32/34in (81/86cm). If I calculate the ease using the above formula it works out as shown in equation B.

This makes for a 34½in (86.25cm) bust, which is absolutely fine if I am trying to replicate a vintage-style garment as it gives us –1½in (–3.75cm) ease allowance.

However, be practical! If, for example, Christmas is approaching and there is a chance that negative ease will become even more negative when you have had your way with the turkey, it may be best to stick with the extra ease and find ways of either shaping your garment or making sure you emphasise certain areas. Also, even if the bust measurement does work out, others may not.

The next section will give you some ideas to help you with your shaping decisions to simulate a closer fit.

B.

95 [number of sts
at widest point]
÷
5.5 [sts per inch]
=
17¼ [inches per side]

The ease of this 1949 jumper has been adjusted from the original 0˝ to 1½˝ (3.75 cm).

Shaping your garment

In the last section we looked at how to work out the actual measurements of your garment, and we made the decision whether to stray into negative ease or retain the shape of our modern pattern. Here we will look at some simple ways to shape your knitwear while retaining some modern comfort.

VINTAGE KNITWEAR SHAPING METHODS

We know that from the 1930s to the 1950s knitwear was worn as a tight-fitting piece of clothing, the closer to the skin the better. Surprisingly, there was very little actual shaping incorporated into the designs, which instead used negative ease, flexible stitch patterns and some clever blocking at the final stages to create a piece that would hug the figure.

Where you do come across shaping, it will mostly be in the following forms:

- A deep, ribbed welt was used to draw the garment in at the waist, and often went further to expand into an inverted 'V'-shape ending just under the bust (see image right).

- Some patterns start out at hip width, decrease at either side in the build-up to the waist and increase again out to the bust width.

- A narrow strip of ribbing at the waistline was a popular method of shaping during the 1930s and 1940s, incorporated into the garment's composition as a design feature.

- Occasionally there was some concession to busts, in the form of a front piece that was slightly wider than the back, or a slightly deeper front armhole.

- Judicious choice of stitch gave the garment greater flexibility, e.g. ribbed panels along the sides of the body stretching from the hemline to just under the arms (see bottom image on page 102) had the effect of making the fabric more elastic and form-clinging. This was a particularly popular feature during the 1940s. The ribbed yoke, another 1940s standard, could have a similar effect on the upper body.

Our modern figures have relaxed somewhat and protest against the smaller shapes (as I am sure even many knitters of those eras did), and our underwear tends to be less structured, so we need to use methods that keep a comfortable fit and still give the impression of a more tailored item.

This classic 1940s jumper uses an inverted 'V' waist welt to accentuate the shaping.

DEEP RIBBED WELT

This is one of my favourite fixes as it is so straightforward (I like an easy life). Patterns with ribbed welts from the 1930s to 1940s could go from a standard 3in (7.5cm) welt to 4in (10cm) or even 5in (12.5cm). As the waistband was actually designed to sit at the waist (rather than the hips, which is more common today), it was a neat way to emphasise that area and nip it in (as shown in the photo right). The extent of your welt adjustments will depend on your original pattern: our example pattern has a shallow welt that I extended to a classic 3in (7.5cm). I included the welt depth in the final length of the garment. You may even want to experiment with the high-waisted inverted 'V' that we mentioned earlier, but make sure you have done some rigorous rib swatching and are sure of your measurements before you do.

If you decide to go for this option, do not forget to look at any other ribbing that is used in the pattern (e.g. sleeve cuffs, etc.) as you might want to reflect any changes here too, to keep a good proportion.

Design No. 490· Price 2ᴰ
KNITTED IN
Sirdar
'SUPER SHETLAND' 3·PLY WOOL

RRAP BROS. (SIRDAR WOOLS) LIMITED • WAKEFIELD

Note the extremely deep ribbed waist in this stylish jumper, again from the 1940s.

WAIST SHAPING: DECREASE METHOD

A 1940s pattern using increases/decreases to shape the waist.

A ribbing stitch is a good way to give your garment a close fit. It was often used in side panels combined with a plainer stitch in the middle to give greater elasticity.

SEE ALSO Darts, page 104, Stitch patterns, page 134

This method speaks for itself: you decrease stitches at either side of the garment in the build-up to your waist, then increase out again in the build-up to your bust. A word of warning: this does require some planning and does not work well with any dramatic width differences – you could end up with unnaturally steep shaping that would look odd and angular.

If you do use this method, consider the following:

- First of all make sure you know exactly where the waist shaping will take place and over what length. To do this you will need to plot out the length of your garment and exactly where your waist sits in relation to it (try sketching it out in your knitter's notebook).

- Make sure you know what your tension is (including row tension) and plot out your decreases and increases accordingly.

To use this method, you first need to calculate how much width you need to lose. For example, you might decide that you would like to lose the positive ease allowance at the waist. If the ease allowance is 3in (7.5cm), perform the calculation given in equation A.

So you will need to decrease your garment gradually by ¾in (1.8cm) at each side, front and back, in the build-up to the waist, and then increase outwards again towards the bust. Now let us translate that into stitches, using an example tension guide of 5.5 stitches/7 rows to the inch (see equation B).

To work out where your shaping should be positioned and over how many rows, refer to 'How to work out vertical dart positioning' on page 105.

A.

3 [number of inches to lose]
÷
4 [sets of increases/decreases]
=
¾in (1.8cm)

B.

¾in (1.8cm)
×
5.5 [stitch tension]
=
4.1 sts [which we will round down to 4]

WAIST SHAPING: RIBBED WAISTLINE METHOD

As I mentioned earlier, this was a commonly used device in some knitting patterns (see image right). If you decide to go for this, be aware that you will need to incorporate it into your overall design as it is a bold feature and has the effect of dividing the torso.

Similarly to the increase/decrease method above, you will need to work out where you want your ribbed waistline to be positioned on your garment. To get the right amount of elasticity, knit up a swatch or two using the main yarn and needles in a k1, p1 rib stitch. Measure your swatch to assess the stitch tension; stretch it slightly when you measure it to establish a realistic tension of how it will fit on you when you are wearing it.

Let us say, for example, that your pattern cast on 107 stitches and your ribbed swatch knitted up to 6.5 stitches to the inch. Let us also assume that your ribbed waistline needs to fit your 30in (75cm) waist, so you need to establish whether or not that rib will sit comfortably. You can work this out as shown in equation A.

So from that final figure of 97 stitches, you can estimate that your ribbed waistline over 107 stitches will give you a comfortable waistline fit with a positive ease of approximately 1½in (3.75cm).

A ribbed waistline is a useful way to add shaping to your garment.

A.

30in (75cm) [waistline]
÷
2 [front and back]
=
15in (37.5cm)

15in (37.5cm)
×
6.5 [rib stitch tension]
=
97 sts

Pro tip

To reduce any 'puff' effect between the hem and waist try using a hemmed edge rather than a ribbed one (see 'Hemlines' on page 150), or a very shallow rib that does not stretch so much using the same size needles as the main garment.

BELTS

I am rather fond of this option as it can be a very effective design feature, particularly if you are using a contrast colour that is also employed in other sections such as a collar, cuffs etc.

You can either knit a belt separately and use a couple of strands of twisted wool attached at the waistline as belt loops, or you could integrate it even more into the design by introducing opening slots into the main garment through which to thread your belt. This is the same method as that employed for vertical buttonholes (see page 153).

Of course you could wear a ready-made belt, but that is not such fun!

This stunning 1930s suit uses a knitted belt to cinch in the waist and prevent the silhouette from looking too tubular.

Darts

Darts can help you shape a piece to the contours of your body; if you want to flare a jumper over your tummy, nip in the waist to emphasise your hourglass or create a closer-fitting bust, a couple of darts here and there will do the trick.

WHEN TO ADD DARTS

As we saw in the previous section, shaping was not something that was commonly incorporated into vintage design, but vertical darts began to make more of an appearance in the 1950s, along with the odd horizontal bust dart, all of which helped to emphasise the bullet bra shape and nipped-in waist popularised by Dior's New Look in 1947.

Since we are looking at modern patterns that will offer more ease allowance, you might want to add a couple of well-placed darts here and there to allude to some vintage shaping, but generally horizontal darts are only necessary where you are dealing with measurements which are proportionally larger than the rest of the body (such as a large bust with a narrow waist).

Before you dive in, I will add a note of caution: since horizontal darts were so rare in vintage-styled garments they could end up detracting from rather than adding to the vintage look, plus they can come with their own problems, particularly where a stitch or colour pattern is involved, so think carefully before deciding.

VERTICAL DARTS

Darts running vertically down a garment give you a way to decrease stitches where fewer are needed (at the waist or leading from the hips up to the waistband of a skirt, for example) and then increase again (for the bust perhaps). They are worked in symmetrical pairs (generally front and back for waist darts) and can give a garment a more tailored look, making them particularly useful for jackets, coats and dresses.

HOW TO WORK OUT VERTICAL DART POSITIONING

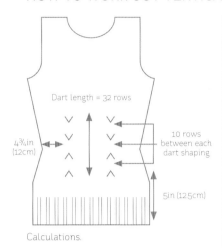

Dart length = 32 rows

4¾in (12cm)

10 rows between each dart shaping

5in (12.5cm)

Calculations.

Let us work out where we want our darts to be positioned and how many stitches will be spanned as follows.

1. First work out how far each dart should be positioned from the side. The measurement between the side of your garment and each dart should cover approximately one quarter of the total front. Taking our modern jumper pattern as an example, we calculate as shown in equation A to find out how far in each dart should be.

2. Next calculate how wide the darts will be. You will need to work out how much you want to narrow the garment. This could be the difference between the garment ease and your waist measurement, for example. Using our modern jumper pattern as a guide, we know that our ease allowance is 3in (7.5cm), so we will work on the basis that we want to get rid of that ease at the waist.

3. Since there will be two darts on each side of the garment, divide the amount you just calculated by 4. In our example that works out as shown in equation B.

4. Translate that width into stitches using your stitch tension as shown in equation C.

5. We rounded down to 4 in the previous calculation because you will always create your darts in pairs over an even number. However, it is also best to work your dart around a central stitch with an equal number of stitches on either side to get a smoother fabric transition, so plan to work your darts over an odd number of stitches (in this case 5).

6. How do we work out how deep the darts should be? Waist darts can be anywhere between 4 to 8in (10 to 20cm) in length. They should be positioned below the bust points and can be placed symmetrically above and below the waistline, or alternatively with slightly more of the dart below the waist than above (e.g. if your dart was 5in [12.5cm] long, plan for 2in [5cm] above the waistline and 3in [7.5cm] below.) The depth you choose can come down to your shape and how dramatically you wish to reduce the width.

A.

19¼in (48cm) [front width]
÷
4
=
4¾in (12cm) [width between garment side and dart]

4¾in (12cm)
×
5.5 [stitch tension]
=
26.73 [round up to 27 – number of stitches between garment side and dart]

B.

3in (7.5cm) [ease allowance]
÷
4 [number of darts]
=
¾in (1.8cm) [dart width]

C.

¾in (1.8cm) [width per dart]
×
5.5 [stitch tension]
=
4.12 stitches
[which we will round down to 4]

7. Using our example, I am going to make my dart approximately 4in (10cm) deep, symmetrically with the same number of dart-shaping rows above and below the waistline. To translate that into rows, I will use my tension guideline again as shown in equation D.

8. Since dart decreases/increases are worked in pairs and I only need to decrease 4 stitches, that means I only need to work two sets of decreases and two sets of increases per dart. The illustration on page 105 indicates how our darts will be made – you can see that there are three 'spaces' in between each shaping row, so to work out how to space out my shaping rows, I will follow the calculations given in equation E.

Since vertical darts are worked on the right side of the fabric, each decrease/increase is counted as being worked over 2 rows so we need to end up with an even number of rows to work our darts over (hence the round-up to 10 rows). This does not always fit neatly into our desired dart length measurement, but the difference in this case is 3 rows over my planned 4in- (10cm-) long dart, which I can live with. So, I will decrease my stitches on the 1st and 11th, then increase on the 21st and 31st rows.

Now we know how far in we want the darts and over how many stitches, let us work out where they should be placed by calculating where your waist sits in relation to the bottom of the garment.

1. Since we know from our pattern that the garment is 23¼in (58cm) long, we need to measure from the point where the neck meets the shoulder to the bottom of the garment and tie a piece of yarn around the torso at that point.

2. Tie another piece of yarn around your actual waist (the narrowest point of your torso) and measure the gap between the two: in my case this equals 7in (17.5cm).

3. Since the dart is going to be 4in (10cm) long, 2in (5cm) of which will fall below the waistline, I know that I need to calculate as in equation F.

I now know that I will start my dart after knitting 5in (12.5cm) in length.

$$D.$$

$$\frac{\text{4in (10cm) [dart depth]} \times \text{7 [row tension]}}{} $$

4in (10cm) [dart depth]

×

7 [row tension]

=

28 rows

$$E.$$

28 [rows available for shaping]

÷

3 [spaces between each shaping row]

=

9.6 [rounded up to 10]

$$F.$$

7in (17.5cm) [hem to waistline length]

−

2in (5cm) [dart below waistline]

=

5in (12.5cm)

Vertical dart instructions

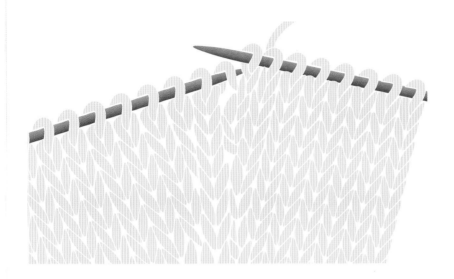

Bearing in mind that for our example we will be working two darts, each one spanning 5 stitches, starting 5in (12cm) from the hem and worked over 4in (10cm), I will work my darts as follows:

Using 3.25mm/US 3 needles, cast on 107 sts. Knit in k1, p1 rib for 3in (7.5cm)

Change to 4mm/US 6 needles and knit in St st for 2in (5cm), ending with a ws row

Place markers on the central stitch of your proposed dart (in our example this will be the 28th stitch and the 79th stitch)

Next row: Work to within 2 sts before marker, skpo, k3, k2tog, knit to within 4 stitches of the next marker, skpo, k3, k2tog, knit to end

Knit 9 rows in St st starting with a purl row

Next row: Work to within 2 stitches before marker, skpo, k1, k2tog, knit to within 4 stitches of the next marker, skpo, k1, k2tog, knit to end

Knit 9 rows starting with a purl row

Next row: Work to the marked stitch, *m1r, knit the marked stitch, m1l*, knit to next marker; rep from * to *, knit to end

Knit 9 rows starting with a purl row

Next row: Work to within 1 st of the marked stitch, *m1r, k1, knit the marked stitch, k1, m1l*, knit to within 1 st of next marker; rep from * to *, knit to end

HORIZONTAL DARTS

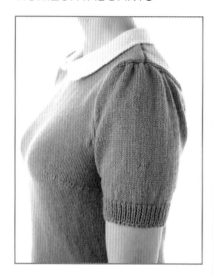

HOW TO WORK OUT HORIZONTAL DART (BUST) POSITIONING

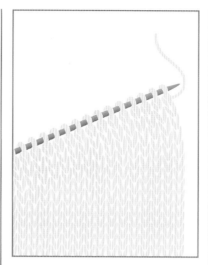

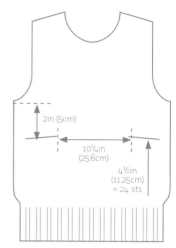

Calculations

Horizontal darts are worked using short rows – that is, you work to within a certain number of stitches before the end of the row, then turn your work to do the same on the other side, and continue working fewer stitches each time.

This is all fine if you are knitting in stocking/stockinette stitch, but they cause disruption in a more complicated stitch or detailed colourwork such as Fair Isle so they are best avoided in more complex designs.

First of all, to work out your bust dart calculations, make sure you have the following measurements to hand:

- Distance between the breast points (this will help to work out the width of your darts; it is a 'no-man's land' into which your bust darts must not stray).

- Garment width measurement at widest point.

- Back length from the base of the neck to the hemline of the garment.

- Front length from the neck–shoulder joining, over the nipple to the hemline of the garment.

The difference between the front and back measurements is an important one. You should know the back length from the pattern guidelines, so you will need to work out where the hemline falls on your body.

In our modern jumper pattern, the guidelines tell me that the length is 23¾in (58cm), so I measure that length out from the nape of my neck at the back and then tie my yarn round my torso at that point. I then measure from the point where my neck meets my shoulder over the nipple to the tied yarn line, which gives me 25¾in (64.3cm). This will help us to work out the depth of our darts, so we will calculate as follows.

1. For the front length, follow equation A.

2. To calculate how many rows we will be working over, follow equation B.

3. I round this up to 18 rows. Since short rows are worked over 2-row 'sets', we will divide that by 2, which gives us 9 short row groups.

4. Next we will work out how much space the 'no man's land' in the middle of the garment will take up. The distance between my bust points is 8¼in (20.6cm), and to that I will add another 2in (5cm) for ease (see equation C), otherwise the darts might look a bit odd if they end up directly on the points. I then subtract that from the total front garment width, which is 19½in (48.6cm). (See equations D and E.)

5. Let us translate that 4½in (11.25cm) dart width into stitches using our tension guideline (see equation F).

6. I will round down the number of stitches per dart to 24. (I have rounded down rather than up to make extra sure that the darts do not creep into the 'no-man's land' area between the bust points). Divide the number of stitches per dart by the number of short row sets to work out how many stitches you will need to exclude at each turnaround (see equation G).

A.

25¾in (64.3cm) [front length]
−
23¼in (58cm) [back length]
=
2½in (6.25cm)

B.

2½in (6.25cm) [bust height difference]
×
7 [row tension]
=
17.5 rows [rounded up to 18]

C.

8¼in (20.6cm) [bust point distance]
+
2in (5cm) [ease]
=
10¼in (25.6cm) [width between bust points]

D.

19½in (48.6cm) [garment width]
−
10¼in (25.6cm) [width between bust points]
=
9¼in (23cm) [width remaining for bust darts]

E.

9¼in (23cm) [width remaining for bust darts]
÷
2 [left- and right-side darts]
=
4½in (11.25cm) [width of each dart]

F.

4½in (dart width)
÷
5.5 [stitch tension]
=
24.75 [number of stitches per dart]

G.

24 [number of stitches per dart]
÷
9 [number of short row sets]
=
2.6 [number of stitches to exclude, which I will round up to 3]

Bust (horizontal) dart instructions

We have already worked out how many stitches to exclude at the end of each row: in our example we will be excluding 3 stitches at the end of the row before turning the work and repeating the same on the other side. In order to avoid any holes appearing, you will need to wrap the yarn around the base of your turning stitch. So we will work our bust darts as follows.

Work to within 2in (5cm) of the armhole shaping.

Row 1 (rs): Knit to within 4 sts of the end of the row. 'Wrap' the next stitch as follows: slip the next stitch on to the right-hand needle purl-wise. Bring the yarn between the needles to the front of the work. Transfer the stitch back to the left-hand needle. Turn the work so that the ws is facing.

Row 2 (ws): Purl to within 4 sts of the end of the row. 'Wrap' the next stitch as above. Turn the work so that the rs is facing.

Repeat the last 2 rows, continuing to exclude 3 sts at the end of each row until the required number of rows has been worked (9 short row groups in our example.)

We are not finished with those wrapped stitches… when you have completed your sets and you come to knit across your short rows, you will need to make sure that when you reach each 'wrapped' stitch, you knit it together with the strand of yarn (lying at the base of the 'wrapped stitch') you used to 'wrap' it to avoid holes forming. Repeat the same on your purl row.

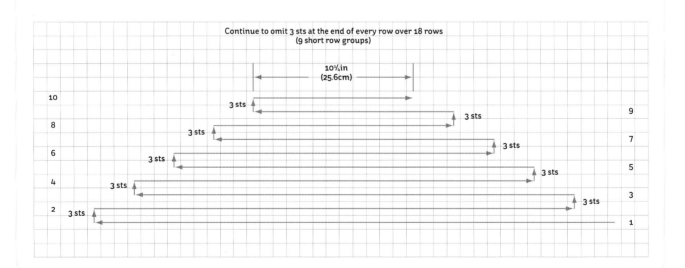

SEE ALSO *Taking your measurements, page 30, Adjusting widths, page 56*

Our modern pattern transformed to give it a vintage look.

Shortening & lengthening sleeves

The ability to shorten or lengthen your sleeves is a valuable asset and can completely alter the look of your garment. Many vintage jumper patterns helpfully gave instructions for both options, offering a flexibility you rarely find in modern patterns – but it is a straightforward process.

SHORTENING SLEEVES

For this exercise you will need to have the following measurements to hand:

- Upper arm circumference (where you want the cuff to end).

- Length from armpit to desired end of sleeve.

A standard short sleeve might start with a certain amount of ribbing, then change to a larger size needle and gradually increase outwards until you reach the shaped part that fits into the armhole. The use of ribbing at the cuffs will prevent the knitted fabric from stretching and lengthening.

Long-sleeved jumpers tend to have longer cuffs than short-sleeved ones to match the length of the ribbed waistband. A longer ribbed cuff on a short sleeve can set the proportions off balance, which is why ribbed cuffs on short sleeves are generally half the length of the waistband welt.

The short sleeve also needs to be more flexible, as the muscles in that area of your arm expand and contract a lot more.

Pro tip

You have a little more flexibility with the cuff design on a short sleeve as it does not have to match a waist rib, so consider experimenting with a different style (see 'Patterns for cuffs', page 130).

Case study: shortening a sleeve

We will use these instructions for a long sleeve as an example, with a stitch tension of 5.5 stitches to the inch using 4mm/US 6 needles:

Cast on 52 sts. Cont in k1, p1 rib for 3in (7.5cm). Change needles and inc over the row to 64 sts. Inc 1 st at each end of the 5th and every following 6th row until there are 68 sts, then on every following 8th row until there are 88 sts. Cont straight until sleeve measures 18in (45cm). Shape top.

Your upper arm is wider than your wrist, so you will need to calculate how many stitches to cast on for your new cuff. You will also need to take into account any ease already applied to the rest of your garment. Let us assume that your actual measurements are:

- Upper arm circumference: 12in (30cm)

- Desired inner sleeve length: 5in (12.5cm).

The calculations given in equations A and B show how to work out how many stitches you will need to cast on; equation C shows how to calculate the number of stitches to increase in the build-up to the sleeve-crown shaping. This means increasing 6 stitches at either end of the rows. Next, let us see how many rows there are to make the increases in the build-up to the shaping. Subtract the ease between your actual armpit and the garment armpit. To do this follow equations D to G.

Revised instructions

Cast on 76 sts. Cont in k1, p1 rib for 1½in (3.75cm). Change needles. Inc 1 st at each end of every alt. row until there are 88 sts. Shape top.

A.

12in (30cm) [upper arm circumference]
+
2in (5cm) [ease]
=
14in (35cm)
[short sleeve hem width]

B.

14in (35cm) [sleeve hem width]
×
5.5 [st tension]
=
77 [number of sts to cast on, round down to 76]

C.

88 sts [number of sts before armhole shaping begins]
−
76 [number of cast-on sts]
=
12
[number of sts you will need to increase in the build-up to shaping]

D.

5in (12.5cm) [innr. sleeve length]
−
2in (5cm) [ease]
=
3in (7.5cm) [actual sleeve length]

E.

3in (7.5cm) [sleeve length]
−
1½in (3.75cm) [ribbed cuff]
=
1½in (3.75cm)
[length available for increases]

F.

1½in (3.75cm) [length available for increases]
×
7 [row tension]
=
10.5 [rows available for increases, which we will round up to 12]

G.

12 [rows available]
÷
6 [number of increase rows required]
=
2 rows [or every alternate row]

LENGTHENING SLEEVES

Make sure you have the following measurements:

- Wrist circumference (where you want the cuff to end).

- Length from armpit to desired end of sleeve.

A standard long sleeve might start with ribbing at the wrist, then increase gradually out towards the desired upper arm width before armhole shaping commences. The increases might occur regularly from wrist to armhole, or they may be worked in two different stages, the first stage to include more rapid increases towards the elbow.

The longer sleeve length needs to take into account some flexibility around the elbow – if you measure the outside length of your arm when it is straight and again when it is bent you will find a difference, and although knitted fabric is fairly elastic, you will need to take this into account for your revised sleeve length.

Unless you are aiming for a loose-fitted style (bell sleeves, for example), you will need to pay close attention to your tension at the wrist. Since most vintage garments were close-fitting, you will not want much ease (a loose wrist welt can look sloppy). You can also get away with a tighter-fitting welt at the wrist than at the upper arm as there is barely any muscle expansion, but make sure it still fits over your hand!

SEE ALSO Taking your measurements, page 30, Adjustment considerations, page 96

Case study: lengthening a sleeve

Let us take the following example of a modern short-sleeved pattern, with a stitch tension of 5.5 stitches/7 rows to the inch (6.5 sts over rib) on 4mm/ US 6 needles, and assume that the sleeve measurement from cuff to armhole shaping is 3in (7.5cm):

Cast on 76 sts. Cont in k1, p1 rib for 1½in (3.75cm). Change needles. Inc 1 st at each end of every following 3rd row until there are 88 sts. Shape top.

We will need to re-plot our sleeve from the bottom back up to the armhole shaping (remembering to take our ease allowance into account), so let us calculate how many stitches we need to cast on to start with.

Let us assume that our actual measurements are as follows:

- Wrist circumference, including 1in (2.5cm) for ease: 7in (17.5cm).

- Length from armpit to desired end of sleeve: 23in (57.5cm).

Calculating cast-on (bound-on) stitches and increases

Follow equations A and B to work out how many stitches you will need to cast on. Equation C will tell you how many stitches you need to increase in the build-up to the armhole shaping.

You then halve that (1 st is increased at each end of the rows) to give you 18 increase rows.

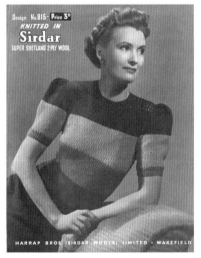

These vintage patterns use different sleeve crowns, or caps, but you could easily adapt them and add some length using the method above.

Calculating where to increase

Now let us see how many rows we have available to make our increases in the build-up to shaping. For this follow equations D to G.

So my revised instructions for long sleeves will read as follows.

Revised instructions

Cast on 52 sts. Cont in k1, p1 rib for 3in (7.5cm). Change needles and increase 1 st at each end of every foll 7th row until there are 88 sts. Continue straight for desired length. Shape top.

If the final calculation had resulted in just over 7, I would have rounded it down to increase 1 stitch at each end of every sixth row, then continued to knit straight until the sleeve measured 21in (52.5cm).

A.

7in (17.5cm) [wrist circumference]
+
1in (2.5cm) [ease]
=
8in (20cm)

B.

8in (20cm) [wrist circumference]
×
6.5 [rib stitch tension]
=
52 [number of sts to cast on]

C.

88 sts [number of sts before shaping begins]
−
52 [number of cast on sts]
=
36 [number of sts needed to increase in build-up to shaping]

D.

23in (57.5cm) [inner sleeve length]
−
2in (5cm) [ease]
=
21in (52.5cm) [actual sleeve length]

E.

21in (52.5cm) [actual sleeve length]
−
3in (7.5cm) [ribbed cuff]
=
18in (45cm) [sleeve length available for increases]

F.

18in (45cm) [sleeve length available for increases]
×
7 [row tension]
=
126 [rows available for increases]

G.

126 [rows available]
÷
18 [number of increase rows required]
=
7 rows

Patterns for sleeves

Sleeve adaptation is something that many people shy away from, feeling it should be left to the experts. It is true that sleeve theory can get a little complex, but if you have the basic pattern already written for you, it is not difficult to make a few modifications here and there.

ADAPTING A SLEEVE SHAPE

The ability to alter your garment sleeve shape opens up a brave new world of options. Puff, box-head and pleated sleeve tops instantly signify a vintage silhouette and are easier to adapt than you would think.

In order to keep things simple, this section focuses on the basic fitted sleeve shape, as this is a great foundation on which to base a few vintage shapes. The basic theory for a fitted sleeve is that the knitted length of the sleeve crown (the area all around the top of the sleeve where the shaping commences) needs to equal that of the knitted length of the armhole shape.

Below you will find some different sleeve shape options. They are based on the fitted sleeve shape so they assume a certain armhole shape (plus the same yarn and tension), which I have provided for our example pattern with different sizing options. Your own pattern may differ depending on the style and yarn used, in which case you will need to adapt your instructions accordingly (see pages 112–115).

A variety of sleeve shapes from the 1930s to the 1950s shows how experimental these vintage designs could be.

Armhole shape

Measurements
32 to 34in (81 to 86cm)
36 to 38in (91 to 97cm)
40 to 42in (102 to 107cm)
44 to 46in (112 to 117cm)
Yarn DK
Needles 4mm/US 6
Tension 22 sts and
28 rows = 4in (10cm)
Stitches at armhole shaping stage
95 [107:119:129]

SHAPE ARMHOLES (FRONT AND BACK)

Cast off 5 sts at beg of next 2 rows
(85 [89:97:107] sts)

Work 2 [4:6:6] rows, dec 1 st at each
end of every row (81 [89:97:107] sts)

Work 8 [8:12:12] rows, dec 1 st at
each end of next and every foll alt
row (73 [81:85:95] sts)

Cont without shaping until armholes
measure 8 [8½:9:9] in (20 [21.5:23:23]
cm), ending with a ws row

8 [8½:/9/9] in
20 [21.5/23/
23] cm

Short set-in sleeve

Cast on 69 [73:79:85] sts, using
3.25mm/US 3 needles. Work in k1,
p1 rib for 1½in (3.75cm), ending with
a ws row

Change to 4mm/US 6 needles and
working in St st throughout inc 1 st
at each end of 3rd and every foll
3rd row to 79 [83:89:95] sts

Cont without shaping until sleeve
measures 4in (10cm), or length
required, ending with a ws row

SHAPE SLEEVE TOP

Cast off 5 sts at beg of next 2 rows
(69 [73:79:85] sts)

Work 8 [10:10:14] rows, dec 1 st at
each end of every row (53 [53:59:57]
sts)

Work 20 [16:16:10] rows, dec 1 st
at each end of next and every
foll alt row (33 [37:43:47] sts)

Work 6 [8:10:12] rows, dec 1 st at each
end of every row (21 [21:21:23] sts)

Cast off 3 sts at beg of next 4 rows
(9 [9:11:11] sts)

Cast off rem 9 [9:11:11] sts

TO MAKE UP

Mark the centre top of your sleeve,
and pin to your shoulder seam.
Pin the rest of your sleeve crown
evenly along the front and back
armhole and sew. If you find there
are any slight differences between
the armhole circumference and
the sleeve crown, try to ease them
in carefully at this stage. If the
difference is pronounced, try
re-blocking your sleeve to gain
some extra fabric. Sew up your
garment and sleeve seams.

Short gathered (puff) sleeve crown

This sleeve starts off the same as a classic fitted sleeve but is slightly wider and continues straight without shaping to give more width at the top (roughly 15 per cent of the upper arm width). As well as being slightly longer, allowing you to 'gather' the surplus fabric, it is also delightfully forgiving as you can adjust the amount of gathering that you have at the top to ease the sleeve into the armhole more easily.

Cast on 69 [73:79:85] sts, using 3.25mm/US 3 needles. Work in k1, p1 rib for 1½in (3.75cm), ending with a ws row

Change to 4mm/US 6 needles and working in St st throughout inc 1 st at each end of 2nd and every foll alt row to 85 [89:95:101] sts

Cont without shaping until sleeve measures 4in (10cm), or length required, ending with a ws row

SHAPE SLEEVE TOP

Cast off 5sts at beg of next 2 rows (75 [79:85:91] sts)

Work 8 [10:10:12] rows, dec 1 st at each end of every row (59 [59:65:67] sts)

Cont straight until sleeve measures 3½ [3.5:4:4] in (8.75 [8.75:10:10] cm) from beg of armhole shaping

Work 12 [10:10:8] rows, dec 1 st at each end of the next and every foll alt row (47 [49:55:55] sts)

Cast off 4 [4:5:5] sts at beg of next 2 rows (39 [41:45:45] sts)

Cast off 2 [2:3:3] sts at beg of next 2 rows (35 [37:39:39] sts)

Cast off rem sts

TO MAKE UP

Sew shoulders. With a needle and your garment yarn, sew a running stitch along the top edge of the sleeve crown. Pull the end of your yarn and gather the sleeve top until it measures approx 2¼ [2¼ :2½ :2¾] in (6.8 [5.75:6.25:6.75] cm). Sew a securing stitch but do not cut off the yarn.

Mark the centre point of the top of your sleeve and pin the sleeve into the armhole with right sides facing. If there is not enough sleeve fabric to fit into the armhole, loosen the gathers at the top a little by loosening the running stitch.
If there is too much, tighten the running stitch. Sew your sleeves into place.

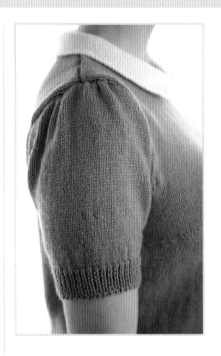

Pleated sleeve crown

This is worked in a similar way to the puff top sleeve with slightly more width at the top (about three times as wide as the final pleated width).

Cast on 69 [73:79:85] sts, using 3.25mm/US 3 needles. Work in k1, p1 rib for 1½in (3.75cm), ending with a ws row

Change to 4mm/US 6 needles and working in St st throughout inc 1 st at each end of 2nd and every foll alt row to 85 [89:95:101] sts

Cont without shaping until sleeve measures 4in (10cm), or length required, ending with a ws row

SHAPE SLEEVE TOP

Cast off 5sts at beg of next 2 rows (75 [79:85:91] sts)

Work 8 [10:10:12] rows, dec 1 st at each end of every row (59 [59:65:67] sts)

Cont straight until sleeve measures 3½ [3½:4:4] in (8.75 [8.75:10:10] cm) from beg of armhole shaping

Work 12 [10:10:8] rows, dec 1 st at each end of the next and every foll alt row (47 [49:55:55] sts)

Cast off 3 [3:4:4] sts at beg of next 2 rows (41 [43:47:47] sts)

Cast off 2 [2:3:3] sts at beg of next 2 rows (37 [39:41:41] sts)

Cast off rem sts

TO MAKE UP

With right sides facing, divide your cast-off sleeve edge exactly into three and form a box pleat by folding the outer thirds inwards. You can either use pins or put a couple of tacking stitches in at this point.

Mark the centre point of the top of your sleeve and pin the sleeve into the armhole with right sides facing. If there is too much or not enough sleeve fabric to fit into the armhole, adjust your pleats accordingly. Sew your sleeves into place.

Box-top sleeve

A sleeve for a great vintage silhouette, particularly popular in the 1940s.

Cast on 70 [74:80:86] sts, using 3.25mm/US 3 needles. Work in k1, p1 rib for 1½in (3.75cm), ending with a ws row

Change to 4mm/US 6 needles and working in St st throughout inc 1 st at each end of 2nd and every foll alt row to 84 [90:94:100] sts

Cont without shaping until sleeve measures 4in (10cm), or length required, ending with a ws row

SHAPE SLEEVE TOP

Cast off 5 sts at beg of next 2 rows (74 [80:84:90] sts)

Work 8 [8:10:12] rows, dec 1 st at each end of every row (60 [64:66:68] sts)

Cont straight until sleeve measures 7¼ [7½ :8:8] in (17.5 [18.75:20:20] cm) from beg of armhole shaping, ending on a ws row

Cast off 20 [21:22:24] sts, knit to end

Cast off 20 [21:22:24] sts, purl to end

Cont in St st on rem 20 [22:24:26] sts for 23 [25:26:28] rows. Cast off

TO MAKE UP

With wrong sides facing, bring the edges of the 'box' together and sew up. Mark the centre of your sleeve and sew it into your armhole.

SEE ALSO Adjusting armholes & sleeves, page 64. Adding shoulder pads to sleeves, page 154

Fitted long sleeve

Cast on 53 [53:55:57] sts, using 3.25mm/US 3 needles. Work in k1, p1 rib for 1½in (3.75cm), ending with a ws row

Change to 4mm/US 6 needles and continue in St st. Inc 1 st at each end of every foll 9th [8th:7th:6th] row until 79 [83:89:95] sts remain

Cont without shaping until sleeve measures 21 [21:21.5:22] in (52.5 [52.5:53.75:55] cm) from the cast-on edge, ending with a ws row

SHAPE SLEEVE TOP

Cast off 5sts at beg of next 2 rows (69 [73:79:85] sts)

Work 8 [10:10:14] rows, dec 1 st at each end of every row (53 [53:59:57] sts)

Work 20 [16:16:10] rows, dec 1 st at each end of next and every foll alt row (33 [37:43:47] sts)

Work 6 [8:10:12] rows, dec 1 st at each end of every row (21 [21:21:23] sts)

Cast off 3 sts at beg of next 4 rows (9 [9:11:11] sts)

Cast off rem 9 [9:11:11] sts

TO MAKE UP

Follow instructions for the short set-in sleeve (see page 117).

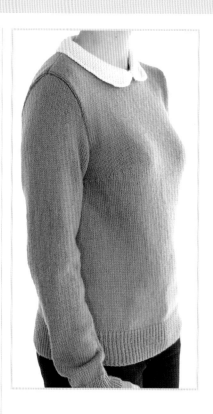

Patterns for collars & necklines

Necklines are more adaptable than you would think, and a pretty collar added to an existing plain neckline is not only straightforward, but can completely alter the look of your garment. Many vintage crew neck patterns adorned their plain neckline with collars, cravats and ties, so this could be just the thing to give your garment that vintage look.

CHOOSING A STYLE

Our modern pattern for the crew neck jumper leaves stitches on a holder at the front and back in order to work a ribbed finish. In this instance I cast off the stitches instead as I find the best results are achieved by attaching the collar separately (it makes it 'stand up' slightly). I also cheated a little by making the neckline a little higher as it was slightly too deep for what I had in mind – have a good look through some vintage patterns to help you decide whether your modern pattern's neckline is appropriate for your re-design.

Each of the classic vintage collars and neckline finishes below assumes a neckline circumference of 17in (42.5cm) (which I have reduced slightly) and a tension of 5.5 stitches and 7 rows to the inch (2.5cm) on 4mm/US 6 needles using DK yarn.

The square and round-edged collar patterns below can both be used on plain or split crew necklines. It is a simple matter to alter a plain crew neck to a split (or open) neckline, which gives you that polo shirt shape so popular from the 1930s onwards.

A pointed collar in a contrast colour (with cuffs matching) lifts this jumper above the ordinary.

This late 1940s/early 1950s square collar is decorated with crochet trim.

OPEN NECKLINE

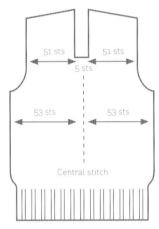

Calculations

1. Decide how deep you want your split – vintage patterns often began the opening as the armhole shaping started, which was roughly three quarters of the garment length, giving it pleasing proportions.

2. Plot the central point in your garment width by halving the stitches. It is useful to have an odd number of stitches at this stage so you can use one central stitch as the dividing point. We will use an example of 107 stitches at the bust width, so our two sides will be 53 stitches with the 54th acting as the central one.

3. Decide on your button band width. This is usually 1 to 1½in (2.5 to 3.75cm). Using your stitch tension, calculate the width in stitches (see equation A).

4. Since we will use one central stitch as a dividing point, the button band will need to span the width evenly either side of this point (see equations B and C).

5. So the button band 'gap' will span 5 sts, and will start 2 sts short of the central point. Using our example where each half equals 53 sts, we will need to knit 51 sts, cast off 5 sts, leave remaining stitches on a holder, continue to work on current 51 sts (see illustration on facing page).

6. At this stage you have three options to add the button band:

- pick up the stitches and knit along the split edge once the garment is completed;

- knit the button band integrally by casting on 5 sts at the button band edge and knitting across these as you continue the rest of the garment; or

- pick up the 5 sts you cast off to create the split and knit vertically (in a rib stitch, for example), attaching the band at the sewing-up stage.

7. The button band itself can be knitted in your main stitch, although if you are knitting in stocking/stockinette stitch, consider a small turned-back hem to firm up the edge. An alternative stitch is usually used to firm up the edge: k1, p1 rib or moss/seed stitch is a nice way to give a firm and attractive button band edge.

8. Continue to knit straight until you reach the neck shaping (remembering to incorporate any armhole shaping as well), then shape the neck as per the pattern.

9. Complete the second half of your yoke, reversing the shaping and remembering to add in buttonholes (see page 153).

The round and square collar patterns on the next page give you alternatives for a plain neckline and a split neckline (in parentheses), as you will not want the collar to overlap the button band on the latter.

I added a rounded Peter Pan collar trimmed with a crochet edge in a contrast colour to our revised modern garment.

A.

1in (2.5cm) [button band width]
×
5.5 [sts per inch]
=
5.5 [rounded down to 5]

B.

5 [button band sts]
−
1 [central st]
=
4

C.

4
÷
2 [halve the amount of sts to span either side]
=
2

SEE ALSO Tension & tension swatching, page 26, Deconstruct to reconstruct, page 32

Round (or Peter Pan) collar

Many vintage jumper patterns were a take on the classic polo shirt with different stitch and colour combinations to ring the changes, so a neat collar could be just the thing to give your garment that vintage look. This collar is worked from the inner edge outwards.

Cast on 98 (92) sts

Work 4 rows in St st without shaping

Next row: k9 (6), *m1, k10; rep from * to last 9 (6) sts. Knit to end (107/101 sts)

Knit 4 rows without shaping

Dec 1 st at each end of next and foll alt 3 rows. (99 [93] sts)

Dec 1 st at each end of foll 3 rows (93 [87] sts)

Cast off

Pro tip

A pretty Peter Pan collar can look great, particularly when you are using a fine yarn. However, the edges can look a little unfinished, so combine this with a crocheted or picot edge (see page 149), or possibly a small hem sewn under.

Pointed collar

This collar is worked from the outer edge inwards and 20 stitches are decreased throughout.

Cast on 117 (112) sts

Work 6 rows garter stitch

Row 7: Sl1, k3, k2tog, knit to last 6 sts, k2tog, k4 (115 [110] sts)

Row 8: Sl1, k3, purl to last 4 sts, k4

Repeat rows 8 and 9 nine times (97 [92] sts)

Row 27: Sl1, knit to end of row

Repeat row 27: four times

Cast off

Collar & tie

The length of the tie is the key thing in this pattern – adjust the length of the middle stocking/stockinette stitch section according to your neckline circumference.

Cast on 16 sts

Working in St st, dec 1 st at each end of every 8th row until 10 sts remain, then work 17¾in (41.8cm)

Inc 1 st each end in next and every 8th row thereafter until there are 16 sts. Work 8 more rows. Cast off.

TO MAKE UP

Fold the straight central section of your collar in half vertically. Match the central back neck to the centre of the collar and pin. Sew centre 17¾in (41.8cm) of straight edge of collar to neck of garment, leaving a small gap free at the front of the neck to ensure the freedom to tie the knot. You may need to sew a couple of stitches to secure the knot.

Work 1 row of double crochet around collar and ties

Patterns for pleats

Pleats are a great way to add decorative vintage detail to a garment, providing a tailored style and finish, while also breaking up large areas of plain knitting. Here we will look at knife and box pleats and pleat effects. You can add volume and a more fluid drape to a garment with knife pleats, or you can use a simulated pleat effect.

Box pleats

Box pleats create a flared effect, making them ideal for the backs of jackets and cardigans to create a 'swing' silhouette. Box pleats can be used singly, but are more commonly used to make a pair of pleats, one facing left and one facing right.

For this example, we will create a set of box pleats that spans 10 stitches. This means you will have to cast on 10 extra stitches when you start knitting the garment. You will also need a spare cable needle to hand.

Knit the required length to the box pleat head. Place a stitch marker at the central point of your pleat.

FOR LEFT-HAND PLEAT (RS)

Knit to within 10 sts of your marker. Place next 5 sts on a cable needle, and place at front of work. Hold the cable needle in your left hand, parallel to the stitches on your main left needle. Pick up the first stitch on your cable needle and the first stitch on your left-hand needle, knit simultaneously through both. Rep with rem 4 sts on the cable needle.

FOR RIGHT-HAND PLEAT

Place next 5 sts on a cable needle, and place at the back of work. Hold the cable needle in your left hand, parallel to the stitches on your main left needle. Pick up the first stitch on your left-hand needle and the first stitch on your cable needle, knit simultaneously through both. Rep with rem 4 sts on the cable needle.

Cont to knit to the end of the row.

Cont in default stitch pattern for the rest of your garment.

Pro tip

The number of stitches you use to span your box pleats will depend on how deep you would like your pleats to be: the more stitches you span, the deeper the pleat, which will give your fabric more movement and a more flared shape.

Knife pleats

If you do decide to go for knife pleats, bear in mind that they are best avoided if you are using a bulkier yarn. You might be able to get away with 4-ply but nothing above… you are better off sticking to 2- or 3-ply.

Knife pleats are created using a slip stitch, and require three times the number of stitches normally needed for the width. This pleat pattern is created over 22 sts.

Row 1: *K9, sl1, k9, p3; rep from * to end

Row 2: *K3, p19; rep from * to end

Rep last 2 rows for desired length

Ribbed pleat effect

Pleats in vintage patterns (particularly skirts) were often a pleat effect created by using rib patterns: this eliminates the bulk created by the extra fabric required to make actual pleats.

Here is a very simple way of making a straightforward pleat effect.

Cast on a multiple of 16 sts

Row 1: *K6, p8; rep from * to end

Row 2: *K.8, p6; rep. from * to end

Patterns for pockets

Pockets are another good way of adding some interest and detail to a plain garment and also giving your garment the look of a particular era, depending on the style you choose. Here we will look at two different pocket styles: patch and integral.

Patch pockets

These are pockets that are knitted separately and attached to the outer garment surface. Unless you have a firm idea of how big you want your pocket to be and where you want to place it, it is often easier to judge this once the main body of the garment has been knitted up. Patch pockets can have a decorative flap, or can be plain with a ribbed top.

Some vintage patterns feature pockets using a different stitch or colour to create a distinctive design detail. Even the plainest of pockets can be used to great effect: one simple 1940s pattern knits the main garment body in knit 2, purl 2 rib, with a pocket in the same rib pattern but placed horizontally.

The following examples assume a tension of 5.5 stitches and 7 rows to the inch on 4mm/US 6 needles using DK yarn.

SHAPED PLAIN PATCH POCKET

Cast on 22 sts, using 3mm/US 2–3 needles, and knit

Work ½in (1.25cm) in k1, p1 rib

Change to size 4mm/US 6 needles and work 3in (7.5cm) in St st

Dec 1 st at each end of every alt row 2 times, then cast off 2 sts at beg of each of next 6 rows

Cast off remaining 6 sts

SQUARE PATCH POCKETS WITH TRIANGULAR FLAPS

Cast on 35 sts for pockets. Work 6in (15cm) in St st

Cast off

Cast on 35 sts for flaps. Work in St st, dec 1 st at each end of 4th and every following knit row until 1 st remains

Cast off

As a design highlight you could knit the pocket flaps in a contrast colour, or in two-row stripes of different colours, as I have done in the sample.

Integral pockets

If you are intending to incorporate integral pockets into your design, make sure you are either using a fine yarn or you have enough ease to ensure that the outline of the pocket lining does not show through the fabric of the garment.

Integral pockets are particularly effective when placed a couple of inches above the breast point, either on one side (the left being the convention) or even both sides. You then have the option to keep it plain, give it a ribbed top – you could also decorate it with a square or triangular flap, or even a button.

1. Decide on the width and depth of your pocket – for this example, 3in (7.5cm) wide and 3in (7.5cm) deep.

2. Work the pocket lining. Cast on 16 sts, work 21 rows St st finishing with a knit row. Break wool and leave these sts on a stitch holder.

3. Knit the front of your main garment per the pattern. With the ws of your garment facing, proceed in pattern until you reach the point where you would like to place your pocket. Take the pocket lining (also with the wrong side facing you) and purl the 16 sts from the pocket lining stitch holder, then continue to purl remaining stitches of the row.

4. Continue to knit the rest of your garment on these stitches (the 16 sts remaining on the stitch holder will be picked up at the end to create a pocket top). Sew the sides of the pocket lining to the main garment in the making-up stage.

For a plain ribbed pocket top, rejoin the yarn and pick up the 16 sts from the stitch holder and knit in k1, p1 rib for desired length.

You could also try a rib variation, moss/seed stitch or other repetitive decorative stitch, or even a contrast colour to highlight a design effect as shown in the example here.

Pro tip

Vintage patterns for cardigans often used a neat way to disguise their integral pockets, by incorporating them into a deep, ribbed waist welt. Make sure your waist welt is deep enough to accommodate the pocket though!

Patterns for cuffs

A good cuff is not only a neat finish to your sleeve, but can elevate an ordinary garment into something more special; a nice, close-fitting one is also the mark of vintage garment detailing. It lends a tailored element to any top or dress and will happily sit on long, three-quarter-length or short sleeves.

CREATING A CUFF

The pattern suggestions below are all based on a wrist circumference measurement of 8in (20cm) including 1in (2.5cm) ease, using a DK yarn, a tension of 5.5 stitches and 7 rows to the inch (2.5cm). If you need to use different measurements, use your tension guidelines to convert the circumference into stitches and adapt the pattern accordingly, following equation A. If in doubt, knit up a swatch or two.

Pro tip

Do not be afraid to experiment with different stitches and contrast colours. You could try a moss (seed) stitch cuff instead of the classic rib. Or maybe where colourwork is included in the garment you could reflect this in a striped ribbed cuff and/or waist welt.

A.

Sts per inch
×
wrist measurement + ease
=
number of sts to cast on

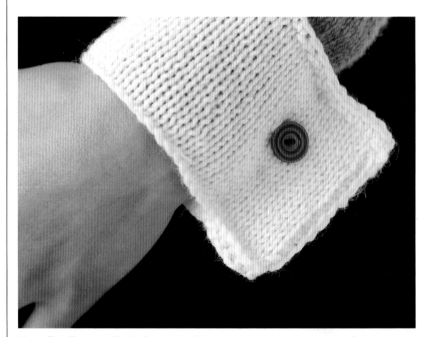

SEE ALSO Shortening & lengthening sleeves, page 112, Patterns for sleeves, page 116

Above: This French cuff with faux button links has been trimmed with a row of single crochet to decorate and firm up the edges.

Right: The contrast stripes in the cuffs of this cardigan are echoed in the welts and yoke.

Classic turned-back cuff

Cast on 44 sts, using 4mm/US 6 needles

Work 3 rows in St st, commencing with a purl row

Next row: K21, m1, k2, m1, k21 (46 sts)

Next row: Purl

Next row: K22, m1, k2, m1, k22 (48 sts)

Cont in St st, inc. as before either side of the 2 centre sts on every knit row until 72 sts are on the needle

Work 2 rows in St st

Next row: Knit forming row for hemline

Next row: Knit

Next row: Purl

Next row: K33, k2tog tbl, k2, k2tog, k33 (70 sts)

Next row: Purl

Next row: K32, k2tog tbl, k2, k2tog, k32 (68 sts)

Continue in this manner, dec. either side of the 2 centre sts as before until 44 sts remain

Work 3 rows St st

Cast off

TO MAKE UP

Fold the cuff in half so that the right sides are facing. Sew one end and along the length, leaving one end open. Turn inside out and carefully sew along the end. Attach to sleeve.

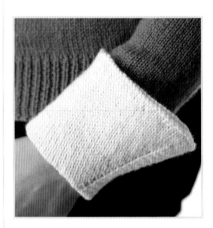

Frilled gauntlet

Cast on 132 sts, using 5mm/US 8 needles

Knit into back of sts for 1 row

Work in moss/seed stitch for 1¼in (3cm)

Next row: K1, k2tog, p1, k2tog; rep. to end of row (88 sts)

Next row: K2tog (44 sts)

Work in k2, p2 rib for 1in (2.5cm), and then change to 4mm/US 6 needles

TO MAKE UP

At this point you can continue knitting your sleeve as you would beyond the end of a ribbed cuff.

Alternatively you can knit in St st for 1in (2.5cm) and cast off, then knit your sleeve separately with a ribbed cuff and attach the frill separately, slightly tucked under the sleeve.

Straight cuff

Cast on 44 sts, using 4mm/US 6 needles

Work 6 rows in garter st

Knit in St st for a further 2in (5cm)

Work 3 rows in k1, p1 rib

Cast off in rib

TO MAKE UP

Sew the sides of the cuff together to make a cylinder. Sew the cuff to your sleeve hem with your cast-off ribbed edge uppermost (so that the garter stitch edge forms the hem), making sure the seams of the cuff and sleeve match up.

Cuff with button 'links' (French cuff)

Cast on 52 sts, using 4mm/US 6 needles

Working in St st, work without shaping until cuff measures 1½in (3.75cm) from beg

Next row: Work 7 sts, cast off 2 sts, work to within 9 sts of end, cast off 2 sts, work to end

Next row: Cast on 2 sts over each 2 sts cast off

Work without further shaping until cuff measures 2½in (6.25cm) from beg

Cast off

TO MAKE UP

Sew cuffs to bottom of sleeves with centre of cuff at underarm seam and 1in (2.5cm) at each end extending beyond sleeve. Sew 4 buttons tog in pairs. Oversew buttonholes in cuffs and insert 'links'. Use a crochet trim (see page 149) to firm up the edges.

Stitch patterns

A decorative stitch pattern can make all the difference to a plain jumper or cardigan. All you need is a knitting stitch dictionary to let your imagination run riot and uplift an ordinary modern knitting pattern into something really special.

CHOOSING A STITCH PATTERN

Vintage designs incorporated many adventurous stitches from lacy designs to cable, and fun, textured stitches such as the bobble stitch, which was particularly popular in the 1930s. In many books from the 1930s to 1950s knitters were encouraged to apply different stitches to their pattern in a 'Ring the changes' section.

Stitches from the simpler end of the spectrum were not neglected either and had a great practical use in the designs of the day: moss/seed and rib stitches were often used to give greater elasticity to the fabric, resulting in a closer-fitting garment.

Some patterns would use a combination of stitches (ribbed side panels, a moss-stitch yoke) as another way to give a tighter fit. I am particularly fond of an incredibly straightforward pattern: stocking/ stockinette stitch interspersed with a raised garter ridge row spaced evenly throughout that results in a simple but classic detail (see image below right).

There are hundreds of different stitches you could use, but here are a few recipes in varying degrees of complexity that can often be found in vintage patterns. The examples were all knitted using a 4-ply yarn on 3.5mm/US 4 needles.

A good look through your vintage designs will reward you with an idea of the more popular stitches used in vintage patterns and how they were used to best effect.

Pro tip

'Extra' stitches do not make up a full pattern, but are 'leads' in or out of the row to centralise the pattern.

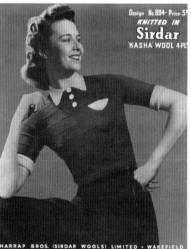

These 1940s jumpers rely on wonderful stitch patterns to elevate fairly straightforward designs.

Embossed leaf pattern

Worked in multiples of 11 stitches over 20 rows, as follows:

Row 1: *p5, yon, k1, yrn, p5; rep from * to end

Row 2: *k5, p3, k5; rep from * to end

Row 3: *p5, (k1, yf) twice, k1, p5; rep from * to end

Row 4: *k5, p5, k5; rep from * to end

Row 5: *p5, k2, yf, k1, yf, k2, p5; rep from * to end

Row 6: *k5, p7, k5; rep from * to end

Row 7: *p5, k3, yf, k1, yf, k3, p5; rep from * to end

Row 8: *k5, p9, k5; rep from * to end

Row 9: *p5, k3, sl1, k2tog, psso, k3, p5; rep from * to end

Row 10: As row 6

Row 11: *p5, k2, sl1, k2tog, psso, k2, p5; rep from * to end

Row 12: As row 4

Row 13: *p5, k1, sl1, k2tog, psso, k1, p5; rep from * to end

Row 14: As row 2

Row 15: *p5, sl1, k2tog, psso, p5, rep from * to end

Row 16: *k5, p1, k5; rep from * to end

Row 17: Purl

Row 18: Knit

Rows 19 and 20: As rows 17 and 18

Wave stitch

Worked in multiples of 8 stitches (+3 extra) over 8 rows.

Row 1: K1, yf, k2tog, k5, *yf, sl1, k2tog, psso, yf, k5; rep from * to last 3 sts, yf, sl1, k1, psso, k1

Row 2: and every alt row: Purl

Row 3: K1, *k1, yf, sl1, k1, psso, k3, k2tog, yf; rep from * to last 2 sts, k2

Row 5: K1, *k2, yf, sl1, k1, psso, k1, k2tog, yf, k1; rep from * to last 2 sts, k2

Row 7: K1, *k3, yf, sl1, k2tog, psso, yf, k2; rep from * to last 2 sts, k2

Row 8: As row 2

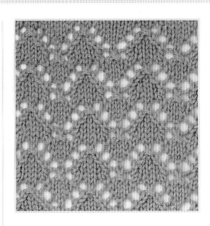

Simple bobble stitch

Worked in multiples of 8 stitches over 8 rows.

Row 1: Knit

Row 2: Purl

Row 3: *k3, make 'bobble' as follows: P into front, back, front, back and then front again of the next stitch (making 5 stitches out of 1), turn, k5, turn, p5, turn, k5, turn, now slip the 2nd, 3rd, 4th and 5th stitches over the 1st stitch to form the bobble, knit into back of 'bobble' stitch, k4; rep from * to end

Row 4: Purl

Rows 5 and 6: As rows 1 and 2

Row 7: K7, *make bobble, K7; rep from * to last st, k1

Row 8: As row 2

Broken moss stitch rib

Worked in multiples of 4 (+1 extra) over 4 rows.

Rows 1 and 3: K1, p1, *k1 tbl, p1, k1, p1; rep from * to last 3 sts, k1 tbl, p1, k1

Row 2: K1, p1, *p1 tbl, p1, k1, p1; rep from * to last 3 sts, p1 tbl, p1, k1

Row 4: P2, *p1 tbl, p3; rep from * to last 3 sts, p1 tbl, p2

Horizontal zigzag

Worked in multiples of 14 stitches over 10 rows.

Row 1: K7, p1, k6; rep to end

Row 2: P5, k3, p6; rep to end

Row 3: K5, p5, k4; rep to end

Row 4: P3, k3, p1, k3, p4; rep to end

Row 5: K3, p3, k3, p3, k2; rep to end

Row 6: P1, k3, p5, k3, p2; rep to end

Row 7: K1, p3, k7, p3; rep to end

Row 8: K2, p9, k3; rep to end

Row 9: P2, k11, p1; rep to end

Row 10: P13, k1; rep to end

Cable stripe pattern

Two stitches for one: this great pattern is a twist on a classic cable. You can use it widely spaced throughout your jumper (maybe four or five bands) leading into the garter stitch stripes at the yoke, or just a couple either side of the garment would be effective. You could also repeat it in the sleeves.

Worked in multiples of 12 stitches over 10 rows for cable, and over 2 rows for stripes.

Row 1: (rs) *p2, k8, p2*, purl required number of sts in between each cable strip; rep from * to *

Row 2: Purl

Repeat these 2 rows 3 times more (8 rows altogether)

Row 9: *p2, cable (place next 4 sts on to a double-pointed cable needle, place at the back of the work, knit next 4 sts from the left-hand needle, knit 4 sts from the cable needle), p2*, knit required number of sts per 1st row; rep from * to *

Row 10: Purl

These 10 rows form one pattern, so repeat for desired length

Next row: (rs) *(p2, k1, sl1, k1, psso, p2, k2tog, k1, p2, purl required amount of sts in between each cable strip)*; rep from * to *

Next row: Purl

STRIPE PATTERN

Row 1: *p2, (k2, p2) twice*, purl required number of sts per 1st row; rep from * to *

Row 2: Purl

Repeat last 2 rows for desired length

Broken rib

Worked in multiples of 6 stitches (+5 extra) over 12 rows.

Row 1: *p5, k1; rep from * to last 5 sts, p5

Row 2: K5, p1; rep from * to last 5 sts, k5

Rows 3–6: Rep 1st and 2nd rows twice

Row 7: P2, *k1, p5; rep from * to last 3 sts, k1, p2

Row 8: k2, *p1, k5; rep from * to last 3 sts, p1, k2

Rows 9–12: Rep rows 7 and 8 twice

Smocking stitch

Worked in multiples of 8 (+6 extra) over 8 rows.

Row 1: K1, *sl1, k2, sl1, k4; rep from *, ending k1 instead of k4

Row 2: P1, *sl1, p2, sl1, p4; rep from *, ending p1 instead of p4

Row 3: K1, *sl next 3 sts on to spare needle, leave at back of work, purl next st, then sl 2nd and 3rd sts on spare needle back on to left-hand needle, leaving spare needle with first st at the front of work; k2, then purl st from spare needle (referred to as 'twist 4 sts'), K4; rep from *, ending k1 instead of k4

Row 4: Purl

Row 5: K1, *k4, sl1, k2, sl1; rep from * until 5 sts remain, p5

Row 6: P1, *p4, sl1, p2, sl1; rep from * until 5 sts remain, p5

Row 7: K1, *k4, twist 4 sts; rep from * until 5 sts remain, k5

Row 8: Purl

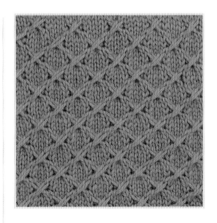

Cross-stitch stripe

Worked in multiples of 10 stitches over 20 rows, using 2 contrasting colours (A and B).

Commence with A

Row 1: Knit

Row 2: Purl

Row 3: Knit

Row 4: *p3, purl the next st, putting the yarn twice around the needle, p2, purl the next st, putting the yarn twice around the needle, p3; rep from * to the end

Change to B

Row 5: *k3, sl the next st, dropping the extra loop (making a long st), k2, sl the next st, dropping the extra loop, k3; rep from * to the end

Rows 6–10: Knit, always slipping the 'long' sts and remembering on the wrong side of the work to bring the yarn to the front of the work when slipping the long sts, and to slip the st pw through back of st to avoid twisting

Change to A

Row 11: *k3, drop the next long st off the left-hand needle and leave in front of work, knit the 3rd st on left-hand needle (the next long st), then knit the 1st and 2nd sts and

sl all the sts off the needle together; now replace the dropped st on to the left-hand needle and knit this st (the crossing of these 4 sts will be termed 'cross'); k3; rep from * to end

Row 12: Purl

Row 13: Knit

Row 14: P2, *p6, purl the next st, putting the yarn twice around the needle, p2, purl the next st, putting the yarn twice around the needle; rep from * to the last 8 sts, p8

Change to B

Row 15: K2, *k6, sl the next st, dropping the extra loop, k2, sl the next st, dropping the extra loop; rep from * to the last 8 sts, k8

Rows 16–20: As row 6

Change to A

Row 21: K2, *k6, cross the next 4 sts; rep from * to the last 8 sts, k8

Repeat these last 20 rows (rows 2 to 21 inclusive)

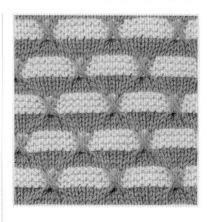

Pro tip

Your choice of yarn will affect the outcome of the stitch pattern. If you are planning to use a different stitch from that used in the pattern, do a swatch. You also need to watch out for any tension differences.

Fair Isle motifs & embroidery

A beautiful piece of colourwork knitting or embroidery can really make your garment stand out. Classic Fair Isle patterns were very popular during the 1940s when yarn was scarce and odds and ends could be used up to make some wonderful designs. A pretty embroidered motif over plain stocking/stockinette stitch can also turn a jumper into a lovely, individual piece.

FAIR ISLE & INTARSIA DESIGNS

You can either use Fair Isle throughout your garment, or you can use it sparingly at the yoke or waist welt, with a matching band at the sleeve welts perhaps. A single motif at the yoke was particularly popular during the 1950s.

If you are feeling adventurous you might want to combine two or three different Fair Isle designs throughout your jumper, although it is best to keep the colour combinations simple if you do this, maybe restricting them to two colours.

You may already have a vintage Fair Isle pattern that you would like to use, but here are a few of my own favourites to get you started. They are adapted from original 1940s and 1950s designs, using shades suggested in the original patterns.

This beautiful 1950s ski jumper uses several Fair Isle patterns in one garment to great effect.

Classic Fair Isle

A great repeat pattern, this is particularly suitable for 1940s-era sleeveless jumpers.

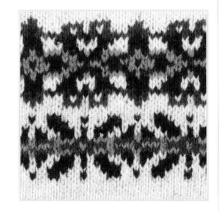

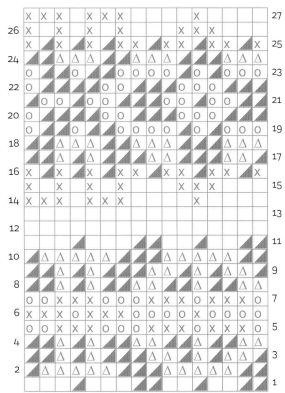

X = Red

O = Green

= Blue

= Neutral

△ = Yellow

Floral Fair Isle

This beautiful repeat pattern is one of my favourites.

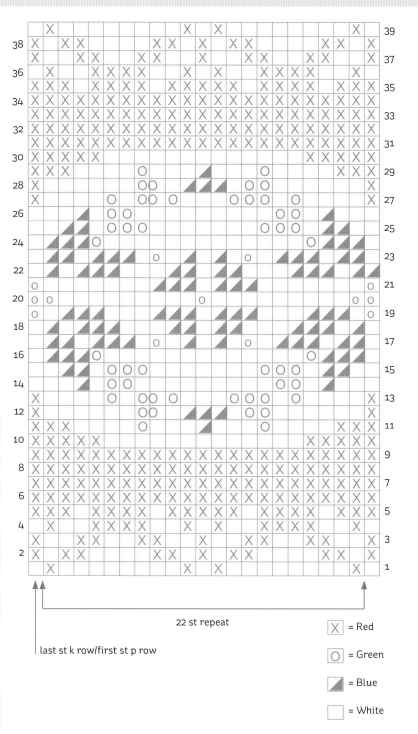

22 st repeat

last st k row/first st p row

| X | = Red
| O | = Green
| ◢ | = Blue
| ☐ | = White

Geometric Fair Isle

This is a particularly good pattern for a border.

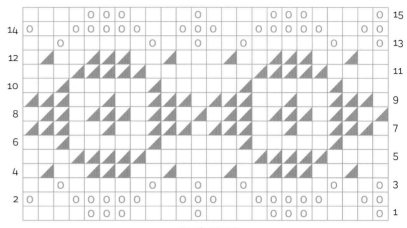

24 st. repeat

O = Green

◢ = Blue

☐ = Yellow

Hearts & bows Fair Isle

A pretty pattern, this is a good one to use on a yoke.

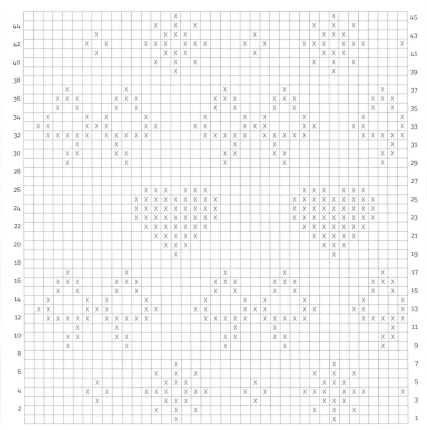

48 st repeat

Cherries Fair Isle

This fun, one-off motif can be repeated on a yoke or either side of cardigan button bands.

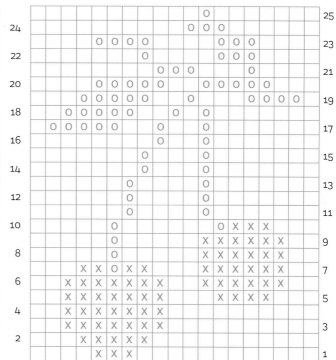

19 st repeat

X = Red

O = Green

☐ = White

EMBROIDERY

You do not have to be an expert with a needle and thread to add some creative details to your garment: simple embroidery stitches such as chain, cross, lazy daisy and stem stitch look great against a plain knitted background. You can even replicate the knitted stitch with an embroidery needle (known as Swiss darning or duplicate stitch), which is effective on an initialled breast pocket (see bottom image, opposite).

You can use yarn for embroidery designs, but it should be slightly thicker than the yarn used for the main garment, e.g. a DK yarn for a 4-ply garment.

Embroidered designs can look particularly effective when they are integrated with a patterned stitch (see image right), although take care not to let the embroidered design overwhelm the knitted pattern or vice versa.

Pro tip

Another commonly used vintage decorative technique was to use small beads or sequins in a pattern or motif. Beads can either be threaded on to your yarn and knitted into your work, or sewn on during the making-up stage.

Integrate your embroidery with a knitted stitch for a great effect: the embroidered flowers in this design are given their own plain background as relief to the rest of the garment's patterned stitch.

POPULAR EMBROIDERY STITCHES

Lazy daisy

Bullion

Long-and-short

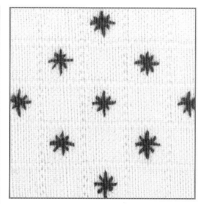

Star stitch

Backstitch

Straight

Herringbone

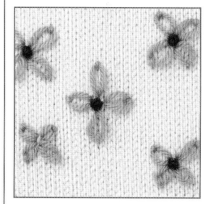

Lazy daisy stitch

Stem

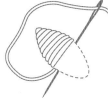

Satin

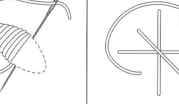

Star

French knot

Buttonhole

Swiss darning (also known as duplicate stitch) is a straight stitch that follows the path of the knitted stitches below.

Contrasting edges & crochet trims

Edges and trims can really give your garment a polished finish. As well as being a practical device to neaten and firm up your knitted edges, a crochet trim is another great example of that extra bit of tailoring that elevates your garment, while a contrast edge is an interesting design device which can echo a colour used in your collar, cuffs, welts or belts.

CONTRAST EDGES

Knitting or crocheting one or more rows in a contrast colour on all outside edges is also referred to as 'tipping'. This technique was used to great effect on front bands, welts, pockets and collars, adding an elegant and simple effect that could completely alter even the simplest of garments.

Giving your welts a contrast colour is incredibly straightforward: simply cast on using another colour, knit the required number of rows and carry on in the main colour. You can even combine it with a crochet trim as I have done with our example jumper.

To add a contrast edge to the button band of a cardigan, pick up the stitches of the final edge and knit four to six rows in garter, moss or rib stitch. You could also continue the edging around the collar.

Design No.825 - Price 3ᵈ
KNITTED IN
Sirdar
'MAJESTIC' WOOL

This stylish 1930s suit is given a tailored feel with its wide bands of smart 'tipping'.

Crochet trims

Try picking up the edge stitches of your garment and creating a simple row of single or double crochet (using the same or a contrast colour), or give one of these slightly more delicate trims a go (see 'Useful resources' on page 160 for links to crochet resources). I have also included a knitted picot edge that looks great on short sleeve hems.

KNITTED PICOT EDGING

You will need to incorporate this hem into the start of your knitting, allowing for multiples of 3 stitches plus any leftovers at either end.

For a 1in (2.5cm) hem, work 1in (2.5cm) in St st, then work a row of holes as follows: k1, m1, k2tog to the end. Cont in St st for 1in (2.5cm).

At this point you can either fold the work in two across the centre of the holes, forming a picot edge, and knit your cast-on edge into the main work (see 'Hemline method 2' on page 150) or continue knitting your garment, fold the work across the centre of the holes and sew the hemline at the making-up stage.

SHELL (SCALLOP) EDGING

Work 1 sc and 2 tr all into the same st, leave a small space; rep to end.

For a larger edging, make 3 tr instead of 2 tr each time, and leave a longer space between.

LOOP EDGING

Work 1 dc into the edge of the fabric then work 2, 3 or 4 chains, according to the desired length of the loop. Leave a space so that the loop of chain lies fairly flat along the edge, then work another dc and another group of chains and so on all along.

CROCHET PICOT EDGING

This pretty picot will give a dainty vintage finish to a collar or hemline.

Work 1 sc Into the first st, *3 ch, 1 dc into the first of these chains, miss 1 st, 1 sc into the next; rep from * to end.

Pro tip

For a simple 1930s sports jumper effect, you could try knitting a couple of bands of contrast-colour stripes at the welt edges. This is also effective when the colours are reflected throughout the garment.

Knitted picot edging

Shell (scallop) edging

Loop edging

Crochet picot edging

Hemlines & button bands

These small finishing details will make all the difference to your garment. Button bands are a useful way to provide a good, firm base against which to attach your buttons. They can also be a nice hidden detail: a piece of contrasting silk ribbon can make you feel good just knowing it is there.

Hemlines

Not every hemline has to end in a ribbed welt; in fact there are times when a well-turned hemline is infinitely more practical. If you are giving your garment some shape at the waist by decreasing and increasing at the edges, or if you are using a ribbed area around the waist, a hemmed edge will prevent any puffing around the shaping. It also looks great with darts, lending the garment a more tailored look, and you can easily incorporate some colourwork to great effect. Hemlines work best when knitted in stocking/stockinette stitch, regardless of the main garment stitch.

HEMLINE METHOD 1

Knit 1in (2.5cm) St st ending in a ws (purl) row, then purl 2 more rows. This creates a natural ridge that will be your fold line. When you make up the garment, fold along the hem and secure it with a light sewing stitch.

HEMLINE METHOD 2

Decide how deep you would like your hemline to be, for example, 2in (5cm). Knit for twice that amount, i.e. 4in (10cm) in our example. Fold it in half and knit 1 stitch from the needle and 1 stitch from the cast-on edge all along the row. Make sure the stitches are matched perfectly to avoid a twisted hem.

Pro tip

Remember that a hemline will not work with bulkier yarns such as DK – since you are doubling up the fabric, the extra bulk will make the hemline too thick.

Hemline method 1

Hemline method 2

SEE ALSO Contrasting edges & crochet trims, page 148, Sourcing & adding buttons, page 156

Right: I used vintage buttons in my revised version of this 1935 design. I had to firm up the buttonholes using buttonhole stitch as they knitted up a little large.

BUTTON BANDS

In the 'Collars & necklines' section on page 122, we looked at different ways and stitch ideas for knitting a button band on an open-necked jumper, which you could also use for a cardigan, but have you thought about the reverse side of your button band?

A strip of ribbon or narrow tape on the reverse side of your garment where your buttons are going to be placed gives your edge a firm finish.

This is particularly useful for press studs, which need a good steady background to prevent the opening from loosening up.

Pro tip

Unless you are familiar with different buttonhole methods, you could also reinforce your buttonholes by adding a band; making a small snip into the backing material and oversewing; or using buttonhole stitch. This does give a fairly rigid buttonhole, so make sure it is the right size.

BUTTONHOLES

Traditionally, ladies' buttons are placed on the left-hand side of the opening. An odd number of buttons is the most attractive arrangement, where possible.

The space between the buttonholes will depend on the design of the garment and the size of the buttons. You could make a feature out of this area, and place small buttons close together (say every four rows).

Make sure they are evenly placed with the same amount of space below the bottom button. You can get away with slightly less space for the top buttonhole, but the button needs to sit comfortably and not rise above the button band.

If you are in doubt about whether or not your buttons will fit the holes, knit up a quick swatch to double-check.

Our revised modern garment uses a button band at the back of its split neckline edges to give a firm background.

Making buttonholes

HORIZONTAL BUTTONHOLES

The easiest way to make horizontal buttonholes is by casting off two or three stitches (depending on your button size) on one row, and casting them back on in the following row to seal the hole.

VERTICAL BUTTONHOLES

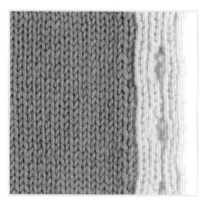

You can also make vertical buttonholes by splitting your knitting and knitting each segment separately before knitting across all stitches to close the hole.

For example, for a button band spanning 6 stitches, K3, leave rem 3 sts on a spare needle, cont to knit for desired length of buttonhole, return to spare sts and knit to match, then knit across all sts.

CROCHET BUTTON LOOPS

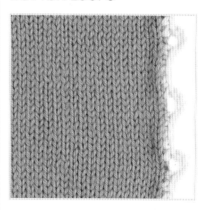

This is a dainty touch that can be incorporated into a nice trim along your button band. Work 3 or more dc, along your edge, then 3 ch, leave a space; rep for desired number of loops.

Adding shoulder pads to sleeves

Shoulder pads were accessories that proved useful during the 1940s to maintain the boxy look of the time. They were easy to make and could be knitted and stuffed with spare ends of leftover yarn. They could also be used to give certain sleeve shapes such as box top and gathered sleeves their defined structure.

CREATING A SHOULDER PAD

If you are planning to add shoulder pads to your garment be aware of the extra bulk they add: if you are knitting a close-fitting garment with very little ease, you do not want the shoulder pad outline to be too visible through the fabric. You will need to make sure your shoulder measurements are wide enough to accommodate the pads, fitting just slightly past the edge of your shoulder if you are using fitted sleeves. They also work very well with puff and box top sleeves.

In theory you can use any thickness of yarn and needles, although obviously the thicker the yarn, the bulkier the pad. Since pads are so quick and easy to knit, you can experiment with a suitable shape and size: if your pad is too bulky, try using a finer yarn and needles.

Here are two different methods for knitting shoulder pads.

The boxy look of the 1940s was accentuated by the addition of shoulder pads to simple fitted sleeves.

Vintage shoulder pads

The most common method of knitting pads in vintage patterns was to knit a square and fold it in half diagonally. They are very common in 1940s patterns and can extend slightly beyond the shoulder into the sleeve crown itself to help to support puff and box top sleeves. As their shaping is a bit primitive they are best suited to jackets and garments with a slightly more generous ease.

This pattern creates a pad that is approximately 2 × 2in (5 × 5cm) before folding and uses 4-ply yarn on 3.25mm/US 3 needles to a tension of 6 stitches to the inch.

Although leftover yarn was often used in vintage patterns, you can also use cotton wool or a sliver of wadding for the actual pad, which will give a slightly more even filling.

Cast on 14 sts and work in St st for 2in (5cm). Cast off. Fold in half diagonally and sew together, leaving a small gap for stuffing

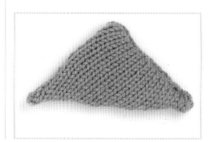

Shaped shoulder pads

The shaped pad is more familiar to us today: its inherent shaping means that it moulds itself to the shoulder and leaves less of an outline.

You can alter the thickness of the pad by using a single layer as it is, or you can make two the same and stitch them together. If you go for the latter, you can then either leave the layers as they are, or stuff them as above.

This pattern creates a pad that is approximately 2 × 2in (5 × 5cm) before folding and uses 4-ply yarn on 3.25mm/US 3 needles to a tension of 6 stitches to the inch.

Cast on 3 sts. Working in gst, inc 1 st at each end of the next row and on every rs row until there are 21 sts, ending with a rs row. Mark the centre st

Next row (ws): Knit to within 1 st of the centre st, slip this stitch and the centre stitch together kw, k1, pass the 2 slip stitches over the knit stitch, knit to end

Cont to inc at each end of every other row until there are 25 sts. Rep the decrease row (23 sts). Inc. each end of every other row until there are 29 sts. Rep the decrease row (27 sts)

Cast off loosely and, at the same time, inc 1 st at each end, casting off after the increase is made

Sourcing & adding buttons

Nowadays there is a lively trade in vintage buttons, sought after by collectors or sewists trying to get that authentic vintage finish, but unless the buttons on your garment are a standout design feature, you can happily buy plain modern buttons and it will not detract from the authenticity of your garment.

USING VINTAGE BUTTONS

There are plenty of times when I have used buttons from my stash, but if they are used on a garment as design features in their own right, it might be nice to find a suitable set similar to the originals. A good place to look is old garments that are too worn out for any other use. The buttons on the 1930s jumper shown on page 151 were unpicked from a 1930s blouse that was beyond repair.

It is often quite hard to date your buttons unless you are an expert, so do not get drawn too far into the authenticity question: if you like them and they suit the garment, go with your instinct.

MAKING BUTTONS

For the thrifty mid-twentieth-century woman, buttons were another thing that you could create yourself, stuffed with offcuts of yarn or covering an older, unwanted button. It is still a nice way to finish off your garment now as you get to choose the colour, size and texture.

Pro tip

Keep your eyes open for interesting buttons. Sometimes I buy buttons that are unusual and store them for future projects.

Vintage buttons have become sought-after, but there are plenty of surprise bargains to be found.

Knitted buttons

One easy way to make your own buttons is use an existing plain, smooth button as a mould and knit a square cover in your desired stitch and yarn (best to use a fine yarn and needles for a fine, firm fabric). Sew a running stitch around the edge, place the button in the middle, draw up and fasten off.

Crochet buttons

Crochet can produce a nice, firm stitch for a button.

SQUARE BUTTONS

Make 7 ch. Work 1 dc into 6 ch, 1 ch, turn and work 7 rows more, taking hook through both loops of stitches of previous row. Fold over to form a square and work 1 row of dc through both edges, thus joining together for three sides. Fill with wool and complete fourth side.

ROUND BUTTONS

Make 4 ch with double wool and medium crochet hook, and join in a ring. Into the ring work 16 tr. Break off wool, leaving fairly long end, and thread into darning needle. Take a stitch into the top of each treble, pull threads tightly together and sew across.

LOZENGE BUTTONS

Working with a medium hook and single yarn, make 11 ch, turn and work 1 dc into each of 10 ch, turn with 1 ch and work 5 rows more, taking hook through back loop only. Sew up one end, fill with wool, and sew bottom and other end.

Tips for finishing

Finishing your hand-knitted garment correctly can seem a little tedious when you just want to get on and wear your new garment, but it is a really important part of the process. Finishing techniques have not altered radically over the decades, but particular methods such as blocking take on more importance with vintage-style garments.

BLOCKING

Since so many vintage patterns were designed to be tight-fitting, it was vital that the finished garment was 'encouraged' to fit the body's measurements. This is achieved before sewing up by pinning out the finished knitted pieces to a board to check the shape and measurements. Blocking is also a useful method to re-shape your existing knitwear if it has lost its shape.

Making a blocking board
You can use an ironing board for smaller pieces, but if you do not already have a blocking board, I would encourage you to make one as follows:

1. Cover a length of plywood with some wadding (a couple of layers of blanket will do).

2. Use a suitable cotton fabric to cover the wadding (gingham is good for this as it gives you a grid for guidelines), making sure you pull it tight to give a smooth finish without lumps underneath.

3. Fasten both layers of fabric at the back of the board using a staple gun.

How to block
You are now ready to block. You will need your original measurements to hand to remind yourself of the intended garment size (you can even pin out the outline of your shape on the board in preparation). Unless you are concerned that the garment is not wide enough, avoid blocking the ribbed welt as this will reduce its elasticity.

I like to start pinning at central points, so I will align the bottom against one of the gingham edges and place a pin just above the welt at the central point, then measure the length of the garment and place a pin at the central neck. The next two pins go at either side of the bust, making sure it matches my intended measurements (stretching very slightly where needed). Continue pinning at regular intervals around

the edges of the rest of the garment, keeping it straight and matching the intended measurements.

What you do next depends on the fibre content of your yarn: your ball band will guide you as to whether or not your garment should be steamed or merely dampened.

Steaming
This is used for most natural fibres and heavily textured stitches (do not use this method with synthetic fibres). Hold your iron about 1in (2.5 cm) above your material and allow the steam to completely penetrate the fabric. Where a textured fabric is used, pinch the stitch into the desired shape. Leave to dry.

You can also use some light steaming on seams once the garment has been sewn together.

Spray dampening
This is the best method for synthetic fibres (if in doubt as to your fibre content, go for this one). Using a water spray bottle, lightly and evenly spray your fabric until it is damp (but not saturated). Leave the fabric to completely air-dry before you remove the pins.

SEAMS

Make sure you use the right technique for the seam rather than deciding that one method fits all. Here are some guidelines as to which technique you should use where (see 'Useful resources' on page 160).

Backstitch

This is the most common method as it is so straightforward. It is a good, solid stitch that will keep your garment held together firmly, but it can create a bulky-looking seam that detracts from the all-important tailored finish. It is best used when the garment is knitted in a fine yarn.

Mattress stitch (or ladder stitch)

This is great for side seams, and particularly useful for matching up stripes and colourwork as it is sewn with the right sides facing. The seam is invisible and can be used on rib, purl and cast-off edges (e.g. shoulders). It also gives a more elastic seam than the backstitch.

Whipstitch/overstitch (or oversewing)

This creates a flat seam that is ideal for joining button bands, collars, cuffs and welts.

Grafting

This gives an invisible seam and is created while the two pieces are still on the needle before casting off.

A well-blocked 1950s jumper uses mattress stitch at the sewing-up stage.

Pro tip

When it comes to sewing the shoulder seams (particularly with fine yarn), try sandwiching some bias binding between the seams before sewing up: this prevents stretching and gives a good, firm shoulder seam.

Useful resources

WEBSITES

www.ravelry.com
Online knitters' community

www.knitty.com
Knitting website with useful tips

www.vogueknitting.com
The last word in stylish knitting,
with great Resources and Free
Patterns section

**http://knitty.com/ISSUEwinter04/
FEATwin04TBP.html**
Knitted sleeve theory

**www.knitty.com/ISSUEfall04/
FEATfall04TBP.html**
Raglan sleeve theory

**www.vogueknitting.com/pattern_
help/how-to/beyond_the_basics/
seaming.aspx**
Finishing techniques and seams

**www.vogueknitting.com/pattern_
help/how-to/frequently_used_
techniques/i-cord.aspx**
I-cord technique

**www.how-to-knit-guide.com/
french-knitting.html**
French knitting technique

www.vam.ac.uk/users/node/1744
The Victoria & Albert Museum's
website of knitting history archives
(plus free 'Victory' jumper pattern
and other free knitting patterns)

www.ivarose.com
Truly astonishing range of
out-of-copyright vintage pattern
reproductions for sale from
pre-1870s to 1940

http://justcallmeruby.blogspot.com
Vintage knitting inspiration

www.nationalbuttonsociety.org
National Button Society

www.tkga.com
The Knitting Guild Association (US)

www.kcguild.org.uk
Knitting & Crochet Guild (UK)

www.whatkatiedid.com
What Katie Did (vintage-style
undergarments)

YARN SUPPLIERS

Adriafil (Italy)
www.adriafil.com/uk

Bendigo Woollen Mills (Australia)
www.bendigowoollenmills.com.au

Brown Sheep Company, Inc. (USA)
www.brownsheep.com

Excelana (UK)
www.excelana.com

Holst Garn (Denmark)
www.holstgarn.dk

**Jamieson & Smith Shetland Wool
Brokers** (UK)
www.shetlandwoolbrokers.co.uk

Loop (UK)
www.loopknitting.com

Marion Foale Yarns (UK/USA)
www.marionfoaleyarn.com

Plymouth Yarn Company (USA)
www.plymouthyarn.com

Quince & Co (USA)
http://quinceandco.com

Sirdar (UK)
www.sirdar.co.uk

Virtual Yarns (UK)
www.virtualyarns.com

FURTHER READING

Brant, Sharon, *Finishing Techniques for Hand Knitters*, Collins & Brown (2006)

Carter, Alison, *Underwear: The Fashion History*, Batsford (1992)

Dorner, Jane, *Fashion in the Twenties and Thirties*, Ian Allan (1973)

Dorner, Jane, *Fashion in the Forties and Fifties*, Arlington House (1975)

Elliott, Sam and Bryan, Sidney, *How to Use, Adapt & Design Knitting Patterns*, A&C Black (2010)

Ewing, Elizabeth, *History of 20th Century Fashion*, Batsford (1974, revised 2008)

Fog, Marnie, *Vintage Fashion Knitwear*, Carlton (2010)

Hartley, Marie and Ingilby, Joan, *The Old Hand-Knitters of the Dales*, Dalesman (1969)

Harvey, Michael, *Patons: A Story of Hand-Knitting*, Patons (1985)

Hemmons Hiatt, June, *The Principles of Knitting: Methods & Techniques of Hand Knitting*, Simon & Schuster (1989, revised 2012)

Ingle, George, *Marriner's Yarns: The Story of the Keighley Knitting Wool Spinners*, Carnegie Publishing (2004)

Matthews, Anne, *Vogue Dictionary of Stitches*, Condé Nast (1984)

Murray, Margaret and Koster, Jane, *Knitting For All Illustrated*, Odhams (1941)

Norbury, James, *The Knitter's Craft*, Patons & Baldwin (1950)

Paden, Shirley, *Knitwear Design Workshop: A Comprehensive Guide to Handknits*, Interweave (2009)

Righetti, Maggie, *Sweater Design in Plain English*, St Martin's Press (1990)

Rutt, Richard, *A History of Handknitting*, Batsford (1987)

Stanley, Montse, *The Handknitter's Handbook*, David & Charles (1993)

Thomas, Mary, *Mary Thomas' Knitting Book*, Hodder & Stoughton (1938)

Veillon, Dominique, *Fashion Under The Occupation*, Berg (2002)

Vogue Knitting: The Ultimate Knitting Book, SOHO (2002)

Watson, Linda, *20th Century Fashion*, Carlton (2003)

Needle sizes

Knitting needle sizes were standardised to the present-day metric system in the mid-1970s, although it took a while for them to filter through to all patterns.

For many years afterwards most patterns referred to the old sizes in parentheses. If you are using metric needles or international patterns, you will need to refer to the useful conversion chart in this section.

You will be needing some rather fine needles – the usual suspects used in vintage knitting patterns are no.9s (3.75mm/US 4) upwards. The size of your needle will determine your tension and yarn choice.

There are references to the fact that WWII period knitters were advised to use dark-coloured needles for light wool and vice versa, which would make it easier to differentiate the stitches in candlelight and the poor light of blackouts and shelters – good advice even today.

In the UK there is a thriving trade in pre-metric needles, particularly some of the novelty coloured plastic ones. Everyone has their own needle preferences: bamboo, steel, wood, etc. I still prefer my mother's old ones that I inherited some years ago, but that is not really due to any purist notions … it is just what I am used to.

Needle conversions

Metric size (mm)	US equivalent	Original UK, Australia, Canada and South Africa
2	00	14
2.25	0	13
2.75	1	12
3	2	11
3.25	3	10
3.5	4	-
3.75	4	9
4	5	8
4.5	6	7
5	7	6
5.5	8	5
6	9	4
6.5	10	3
7	10.5	2
7.5	11	1
8	12	0
9	13	00
10	15	000

Measurement conversions

Imperial	Metric
1/8in	3mm
3/8in	1cm
1in	2.54cm
12in (1ft)	30cm
1yd	91.44cm
1yd 3in	1m

Weight conversions

Imperial	Metric
1oz	28g
1lb (16oz)	450g
2lb 3oz	1kg (1,000g)

Equipment

You will be familiar with the usual knitter's toolbox, but I have listed below some particularly essential items required by the vintage knitter.

KNITTING

Knitting needle gauge
An essential part of your vintage knitting kit so that you are easily able to find the modern-day equivalent needles.

Cable needles
Not only used for cable knitting and Fair Isle projects (or stranded knitting), but also very useful to have one on hand for picking up very fine stitches you may have dropped further back in your knitting.

Crochet hooks
Many vintage patterns use a bit of crochet round the edges for finishing – remember to check the 'Materials' section of your pattern in your initial assessment as it is not always obvious from the pattern cover image.

Stitch markers
Never referred to in vintage patterns (my mum and nans used a scrap of different-coloured wool), but a nice piece of kit available nowadays in a cornucopia of choices to mark your place in complicated stitch patterns.

Row counters
A row counter can help you keep track of which row you are working on – also extremely handy for complicated stitch patterns and Fair Isle.

Sewing needles
Blunt-ended darning needles are used for sewing your garment up in the final stages. Also for embroidering motifs on to your garment using a Swiss darning stitch (see 'Embroidery', page 146).

GENERAL

Pins

Used for pinning your garment together at the making-up stage, and also as a marker for measuring tension squares. I find dressmakers' pins with coloured ends preferable as they are easy to spot when you are removing them.

Tape measures

Dressmakers' flexible tape measures are preferable for taking your body measurements, whereas rigid measures or rulers are better for measuring tension swatches.

Scissors

A small pair of sharp scissors is a good addition to your toolkit for snipping off the ends of yarns.

Graph paper

Used to mock up shapes, motifs and colourwork, where each square represents a stitch. Bear in mind that if you use graph paper with absolute square measurements, this will not give you an accurate representation of your row tension versus your stitch tension (stitch tension is usually less than your row tension).

Dressmakers' spot-and-cross paper

This, and other gridded pattern-cutting papers, are very useful for making up a life-size pattern of the original garment, which you can then use to plan your re-sized project.

Calculator

Essential for working out pattern adjustments – keep one in your knitting bag or with your notebook for translating tension swatch measurements into stitch quantities.

Notebook or sketchbook

Get into the habit of keeping as many notes as you can about your projects for future reference. Include tension swatches, stitch examples, yarn possibilities, as well as sketches and re-sizing notes.

Glossary of UK & US terms

Knitting is a surprisingly international language, but some terms differ and do not always translate so well across the oceans, so I have included a few explanations below.

armhole/armscye: the 'hole' in the top part of the bodice into which the sleeve is fitted. The term is believed to have been abbreviate from the phrase 'arm's eye'.

cast off/bind off: the last row of knitting, worked to remove the fabric from the needle; it also defines the edge of your knitted fabric.

cast on/bind on: create the first row of stitches when knitting.

tension/gauge: a form of measuring how many stitches and rows are knitted to the centimetre or inch. In the UK 'gauge' is used to refer to needle sizes.

DK (double knitting)/light worsted: the finest of the Medium-weight yarn categories and the most popular. Also referred to as Light Worsted.

garter stitch/plain: knit every row.

stocking stitch/stockinette: knit 1 row, purl 1 row, abbreviated to St st.

moss stitch/seed stitch: a textured stitch whereby you knit 1 stitch, purl 1 stitch and continue for the rest of the row. The knit and purl stitches are alternated on the following row, creating a raised stitch effect.

jumper/sweater: the word 'sweater' is widely recognised; in the UK 'jumper' is the more common term, but this is not as familiar elsewhere.

General glossary

1 x 1 rib/k1, p1 rib: a means of creating a rib stitch; 1 stitch is knitted, one stitch is purled and so on. Can be extended to 2 x 2 rib, 3 x 3 rib, etc.

ball band/belly band: the outer packaging band or label on balls or skeins that gives information about the yarn (tension, yardage, etc.).

colourwork: a knitting technique using two or more colours.

drape: this refers to the ease and flow of movement in a garment. Needle sizes and yarn weights affect drape: a fine needle and medium-weight yarn might create a garment with little flow; a thick needle and fine yarn will create a lacy garment with little structure.

Fair Isle: a form of colour pattern knitting that traditionally uses at least two colours in a row, carrying the yarn not being used at the back of the work. Also referred to as 'stranded' knitting.

fingering: a Fine-yarn weight equivalent to a 4-ply yarn.

intarsia: a form of colour pattern knitting in which each motif is worked individually using separate strands of yarn (unlike Fair Isle).

light fingering: a Fine-yarn weight equivalent to a 3-ply yarn.

ply: the twisting together of two or more strands. The term is also used to describe a yarn weight.

skein: a length of yarn wound into a long coil as opposed to a ball.

sleeve crown: the top of the sleeve, from where the shaping begins.

stitch definition: the clarity or visibility of a knitted stitch.

welt: a strengthening or ornamental finish at the edge of a garment to prevent stretching (e.g., the ribbed section at the bottom of a garment or sleeve).

wraps per inch (WPI): a method of measuring a yarn gauge by wrapping the yarn thread around the distance of an inch. The number of threads covering the inch is the total wpi. The more threads over the inch, the finer the yarn gauge; the fewer threads, the heavier.

yardage/meterage: the number of yards or metres in a ball or skein of yarn. Use this to help determine how much yarn you require for a knitted item, or the weight of a yarn.

Abbreviations

alt	alternate		p	purl
beg	beginning		p1	purl 1 stitch
dec	decrease		p2 tog	purl 2 stitches together
foll	following		patt	pattern
gst	garter stitch (every row knit)		psso	pass slip stitch over
inc	increase		pw	purlwise
k	knit		rem	remaining
k1	knit 1 stitch		rep	repeat
k2tog	knit 2 stitches together		rs	right side
kw	knitwise		st	stitch
m.st.	moss stitch		sts	stitches
m1	Make a stitch by picking up and knitting the loop lying between the stitch just knitted and the next stitch		skpo	slip 1 stitch, knit 1 stitch, pass the slipped stitch over the knitted stitch (sometimes written as s1, k.1, psso)
M1R	Make a stitch by inserting your left needle into the loop lying in front of the next stitch from back to front, then knit into the front of the stitch (knitwise). Creates a '/' shape for darts		sl1	slip one stitch
			St st	stocking stitch (one row knit, one row purl)
M1L	Make a stitch by inserting your left needle into the loop lying in front of the next stitch from front to back, then knit into the back of the stitch. Creates a '\' shape for darts.		tbl	through the back of the loop
			yon	yarn over needle
			yrn	yarn around needle
			ws	wrong side
			yfwd	bring the yarn forwards

How to create knitter's graph paper

You can identify any potential revisions to a garment by using your tension swatch and the garment's actual measurements, then plotting it all out on knitter's graph paper. This is particularly useful for sleeve crowns (caps). Knitter's graph paper can be created using spreadsheet software (there are freeware versions available). You will use each cell to represent one stitch, so you will need to make sure it is the right height and width, as follows. As an example we will use a tension swatch of 7 sts/10 rows per inch (2.5cm).

1. First calculate your tension over 10cm (it is easier to work using centimetres) : 28 sts/40 rows = 10cm

2. To calculate the height of your cell (row height) divide 10 by your row tension: 10 ÷ 40 = 0.25

3. To calculate the width of your cell (stitch width) divide 10 by your stitch tension: 10 ÷ 28 = 0.35

4. Open your spreadsheet software. In the far left-hand corner of the spreadsheet (above the numbered rows, alongside the lettered columns), you will see a blank rectangle; click on this to highlight the whole spreadsheet.

5. From the top menu, click on Format > Row > Height. Adjust to 0.25.

6. Next, click on Format > Column > Width. Adjust to 0.35.

7. Give your cells a border, select your print range and off you go!

The formatting Menu location may vary in different applications, but you should be able to find it pretty easily. If you want to create a full-scale pattern of your document, stick the pages together at the back, making sure you match up the grid correctly.

Index

Acknowledgements

This book is for those clever knitters in my family: my mum, Pamela; both grandmothers, Lilian and Elsie; and sister Stephanie, who patiently taught me how to knit and crochet, picked up endless dropped stitches and provided the original, stylish inspiration for my vintage knit love.

Loving thanks to those close to me who put up with me during the writing of this book: to Roger for his encouragement and support, to Brenda for helping me squeeze out extra time and of course to Lucas who generously shares so much of his time spent with me alongside my needles and yarn. Also, I could not have done this without Talwinder and Sibilla, who listened to me drone on endlessly about knitting and scribbling.

I am unbelievably grateful to Isheeta, Lindy and Emily at RotoVision for their unflagging support, for sharing a vintage vision and, above all, for taking a punt on me. Thanks also to Judith for her clear-headed guidance, and the talented Julia for testing the patterns.

Those excellent yarn harbingers, Coats UK, Wendy and especially Sirdar, have been invaluable in allowing us permission to use their wonderful archive images and plunder their incredible heritage. Special thanks too to Peggy at Iva Rose and Kelly Smith for helping me track down hard-to-find images.

Thanks too to Thomas B. Ramsden & Co (www.tbramsden.co.uk) for granting us permission to use the lovely Wendywear pattern image (No. 429).

Here is to a couple of wonderful knitters whose fervour inspired me to take the plunge: Susan Crawford for her style, passion and inspiration, and Loraine McClean for her knowledge and wonderful enthusiasm. Thanks too to that clever vintage knitter Anne Finch at that treasure trove otherwise known as the High Street Retro Centre in Hastings (East Sussex), some of whose beautiful garments appear in these pages.

I am indebted to Liz and Kevin at The Shop in Lewes (East Sussex), for their amazing taste and for allowing us to photograph their beautiful shop; to Clare at The Buttercup for the loan of her gorgeous cafe and supplying us with the finest cake; and, of course, to our beautiful models Faith, Rebecca and Sam, not forgetting the lovely Jen (excellent multi-tasking there).

Talking of photography, thanks to Ivan Jones for his creative talents and for bringing these twentieth-century designs back to life.

Of course this book would never have been written without those talented and adventurous unsung knitwear designers from the 1930s, 1940s and 1950s, who keep me falling in love deeper every day.

About the author

Geraldine Warner has been knitting and crocheting since the age of seven, taught by her mother and grandmothers who instilled in her a love of vintage knitting patterns.

Over the years she has developed a style of her own, adapting these wonderful designs for a modern fit and yarn choice.

She has worked at the creative end of the media and digital marketing industries, but knitting has always been her first love. In her spare time she likes to write about the evolving possibilities of modern and vintage at her Skiff Vintage Knitting blog.

Geraldine lives in Lewes, East Sussex, with her husband, young son, and a collection of cats and dogs.